LET'S GET RID OF

SOCIAL SECURITY

HOW AMERICANS
CAN TAKE CHARGE
OF THEIR OWN FUTURE

E. J. MYERS

 **Prometheus Books**

59 John Glenn Drive
Amherst, NewYork 14228-2197

Published 1996 by Prometheus Books

00 99 98 97 96   5 4 3 2 1

Library of Congress Cataloging-in-Publication Data

Myers, E. J. (Edwin J.)
    Let's get rid of social security : how Americans can take charge of their own future /
E.J. Myers.
        p.   cm.
    Includes bibliographical references.
    ISBN 1–57392–015–0 (hc : alk. paper)
    1. Social security—United States. I. Title.
HD7125.M887   1996
368.4′3′00973—dc20
                                         95–47520
                                           CIP

Printed in the United States of America on acid-free paper

Dedication

To my beloved daughter, Barbara, one of the finest people that the good Lord ever put on the face of this earth. Her gentle soul and indomitable spirit in the face of adversity is an inspiration to us all.

Foreword

Ed Myers is a small businessman with a large dose of horse sense to offer Washington. He has come up with the outlines of a solution to the biggest problem confronting democracy: the government's failed campaign to replace private saving with public spending.

Myers recognizes that Social Security is going over a cliff and could drag our future down with it. Government projections suggest that the combined cost of promised old-age benefits under current law could soar to nearly half of the total U.S. payroll in the early decades of the next century. Worse yet, these programs discourage savings by driving up deficits and relieving intended beneficiaries of the need to accumulate the wealth that otherwise would be necessary to produce the same income stream through investments.

Moreover, even if America's young wanted to save, soaring Social Security taxes make it much tougher for them to do so. Finally, by depleting the nation's savings pool, Social Security makes it more costly for business to expand, and in so doing, creates a "giant sucking sound" when assembly lines for products like microwaves and VCRs, which were invented here, go abroad in search of lower capital costs. The result is a vicious circle of lower incomes, slow economic growth, and declining savings.

Myers would end these deadly threats by turning our welfare-based social security system into one funded by an explosion of personal savings. He would eliminate the regressive transfers that now occur when waitresses and construction workers are taxed to subsidize the greens fees of retired doctors and accountants. And he would revitalize two of the values that made America great: personal thrift and the civic responsibility we all share not to become dependent on government subsidies.

Ed Myers urges a return to basic values. His book is a roadmap to social, cultural, and economic renewal, full of refreshing, common-sense advice for policy makers. It turns out that the solution to America's biggest problem is fairly straightforward. Every member of Congress should read this book and reflect.

Paul Hewitt, Vice President
National Taxpayers Union Foundation

Acknowledgments

This book could not have been written without a great deal of help from many people. They gave freely of their advice, time, and know-how to see this project succeed. My thanks to all of them.

A special thank you to Congressman Bill Archer, R-Texas, and his staff, both in Houston and Washington, for all their help in researching this project. Several in particular: Karen Worth, now retired and formerly Minority Social Security Council in Washington, helped immensely with the research and by permitting me to tap her vast knowledge of the Washington scene. Later on Valerie S. Nixon, Subcommittee Staff Director, went out of her way many times, in spite of her heavy load of responsibilities, to furnish me with the research that was needed. Finally Geoffrey C. Kollmann of the Library of Congress supplied many Congressional Research Service reports and was the first to evaluate this concept in a positive way.

Paul Hewitt, Vice President, National Taxpayers Union Foundation was a terrific help. A leading expert in this field, and also of the ways of Washington, he gave freely of his time and considerable knowledge. In reviewing my early writings with a straightforward approach he kept me going in the right direction. The undertaking would have been a great deal harder without his efforts.

Ray Pederson, Managing Editor of the *Houston Chronicle* was most helpful in allowing me to use many articles for reference. In addition, I would like to thank Associate Editor Frank Michel and *Outlook* Editor David Langworthy for publishing a number of articles that helped me get this message to the public. I owe all of them a large vote of thanks. In the past year the nonfiction corner of the Manuscriptors Guild of Houston helped a great deal in critiquing the various chapters.

Then a very special vote of thanks is owed to my editor, Steven L. Mitchell, editor-in-chief of Prometheus Books, for all his help. He understood the idea and in his unique way smoothed the rough edges to make sure this story was told so that all Americans could read and understand what the future holds.

A large debt is owed to Robert J. Myers, former chief actuary of Social Security, and Dr. Herman Harrison, Ph.D, a renowned computer physicist, for validating the various tables and schedules in Part Three.

Larry Forehand, president of Casa Olé Mexican Restaurants; Steve Schneider, president of Interpax; and Ralph Block, a distinguished and outstanding stockbroker for A.G. Edwards & Co. all gave me immense help and encouragement. They believed in this concept and went out of their way to help.

Don Kebodeaux of First Financial Capital and Rick Gornto of First Financial Benefits also added a dimension that validated this concept in a very unique way. They had been quietly demonstrating, for nearly two decades, that this concept works, and works very well, in three south Texas counties. Former County Judge Ray Holbrook of Galveston was most kind and helpful in relating the start of the Galveston plan and its great success. These counties of south

Texas owe these three dedicated men a great deal for their wisdom and foresight. Their success can be a guiding light to all America.

My agent, Mike Doran, worked diligently for two years to bring this project to a successful conclusion. His professional expertise proved to be invaluable.

Finally without a doubt, the help and guidance of my beloved wife, Sally, made all of this possible.

Contents

Foreword by Paul Hewitt   7

Acknowledgments   9

Introduction   15

PART ONE: THE SOCIAL SECURITY MESS
           AND HOW IT GREW

1. Introduction to Folly: The Band-Aid Approach   21
2. The Monster Grows While Congress Dithers   33
3. What Franklin Roosevelt Really Wanted   45
4. Social Security Today   57
5. Baby Boomers on the Way to Bust   73

6. The Amazing, Vanishing Trust Fund Surplus   87

7. The Independent Agency Question   101

PART TWO: THE COLOSSAL PRIVATE
PENSION DEBACLE

8. A Short History of Pension Plans   115

9. The Pension Benefit Guaranty Corporation   127

10. Federal Government Retirement Plans   141

11. State Retirement Systems   155

12. Where Do We Go from Here?   167

PART THREE: THE REVOLUTION THAT MUST COME

13. The Solution Begins: The Window of
     Opportunity Is Here!   175

14. The Beginning of New Ideas   185

15. The Individual Security Retirement Account   201

16. Funding Current Social Security   217

17. The Social Security Investment Banking Corporation 235

18. Public Ownership of the SSIBC   247

19. The Win-Win Results   253

Glossary   259

Bibliography   265

Index   267

Introduction

Thirty-five year old Jane Rogers sat quietly at her computer. It was the first such moment in days. She had finally seen her boss off on his trip to Washington and for once it looked like he had remembered everything. Just perhaps, he and the rest of the group could get some of those congressmen to listen.

Jane knew these moments would not last very long. By mid-morning the staff would be bringing in the weekly reports. In this lull her mind wandered to Casper, Wyoming, where her folks now lived. That $91 a month, one bedroom apartment that Mom and Dad lived in wasn't a palace, but it sure was a lot better and much easier on the pocketbook than what they could get living near her in Houston.

Tom and Mary Henderson, ages eighty-two and seventy-five respectively, were people of the land. Jane's folks had spent a good part of their lives as farmers and ranchers, and through it all they had managed to raise and nurture six children who were now scattered throughout the country. Tom had spent a short period of time in the oil fields as a roughneck, but really didn't like it and had gone back to ranching.

In 1964, Tom and Mary came to Houston to live, and that made Jane, the youngest of the six children, very happy. Tom worked as an independent carpenter, and being self-employed, he paid both the employee's and the employer's share Social Security tax.

Tom never quite understood this, but since President Roosevelt had led the country through the dog days of the Great Depression and had started Social Security, he thought it must be all right. Who was he to question the judgment of all those senators and congressmen in Washington. That's why we sent them there. Besides, everyone said Social Security will take care of us in our elder years.

In 1981 the rude awakening came. The years had taken their toll and Dad wanted to retire. Two carotid artery operations and two triple bypasses had only hastened the day.

Jane made the necessary arrangements and on the appointed day she took her parents to the Social Security office. She remembered that day with a good deal of bitterness and distress. After much heated discussion about Tom's jobs and Social Security payments, the annoying, self-righteous clerk curtly advised the Hendersons they would receive not quite $500 per month.

The crestfallen Hendersons could hardly believe their ears. Jane was speechless. Is this what President Roosevelt had in mind? Why had all those Democrats in Congress—the politicians we believed in—been telling everyone for forty years that Social Security would take care of things in a person's retirement? Believing in politicians is like stepping into quicksand.

Jane knew it meant that Mom and Dad would have to move back to Dad's birthplace, Casper, Wyoming, even though the winters there could be pretty hard. At least there the Social Security money would go a little farther, and with what she and her brothers could send they could at least survive.

Jane had heard many times that Social Security was going broke and wondered what was happening to all those billions of dollars that everyone was and is paying into the system. If this was what she and her children had to look forward to, then a big change was needed in Washington.

The tragedy of it is that the Hendersons and many other hard-working Americans have sent all those men and women to Congress to plan for the future, not to make hollow promises and pay lip service to their constituents. Technically the Social Security bureaucrats may have been right in this case according to its existing rules, but there can be no doubt that the current system is unable to handle the problems it faces. Unfortunately it is too late to do much for the current recipients, but it's a different story for future generations.

Jenny Jones graduated from high school and went on to be an assistant bookkeeper at the local utility company. Two years later she met Dan, who had just been mustered out of the army, and six months later they were married. During the next four years they had two children. Jenny stayed home to raise the youngsters, an arrangement that she and Dan had thought was the right thing to do. A year later Dan was killed one afternoon in an accident while driving the company truck.

With two young children Jenny decided to stay home and see to their upbringing. She applied for Aid to Families with Dependent Children (AFDC), a welfare program administered by the Social Security Administration, with funds coming from Congressional appropriations, and moved into low-cost housing. As each child grew up and reached the age of eighteen, the money stopped.

Not having worked in well over a decade, Jenny had to settle for whatever job she could find. Working at various low-paying jobs she managed to survive. At age sixty-two she applied for Social Security, but much to her surprise she learned she would only receive $450 per month.

Is this what we envisioned? Has the Social Security system somehow gone awry? Did the system help a young mother or was she doomed to living off the public dole?

If this young mother had gone back to work and had the Social Security withholding tax taken out of her paycheck each week been invested in a retirement plan based on income and growth, where would she be today? The answers would surprise you.

It's great to lend a hand, but we should be very careful how we do it. America was built on individual drive and ambition, not on the government taking care of us for life.

As with each coming spring, when life begins anew from the ashes of yesterday, so it can be with Social Security. From the trials and tribulations of the past there can evolve a sound and secure retirement for our children and grandchildren, based on investment and growth. The idea that big government can take care of everyone has been shown to be an illusion and no longer valid. The Social Security taxes paid by individuals and employers are now so high that any further increases will make them very regressive in nature and cause untold problems. All the necessary pieces are now in place to bring Social Security into the twenty-first century, making it a truly great retirement system.

Transforming Social Security will take an act of Congress, but it is up to us to demand action and show our legislators what we expect of them.

I wrote this book to show that there is a way, a very good way, to take charge of our future.

PART ONE

The Social Security Mess
and How It Grew

1

Introduction to Folly:
The Band-Aid Approach

In the years immediately following the end of World War II, the United States was unquestionably the most robust political and economic power the world had ever known. Of the Allies who had beaten the Axis powers, the United States was the only major power spared the horror of experiencing the war firsthand, on its own soil. Unlike England, France, Germany, and the Soviet Union, our industrial and communications infrastructure had not been destroyed or seriously damaged. This factor, plus the tremendous surge of effort, belt-tightening, and reinvestment through the war years left in place a tremendous pent-up drive of production capacity once the fighting was over. The United States would for the better part of a generation seem like an economic and political juggernaut that nothing could ever touch, not even the inevitable reality of history's cycles.

The returning American soldiers found that the country and their way of life had changed in ways which only gradually became clear. For one thing, the millions of women on the home front who had made possible high rates of war machinery production while the men were away would never again be entirely satisfied to return to hearth and home now that they had tasted the financial rewards and personal satisfaction of their work efforts. It was just not in the cards. They and their daughters would help energize the rising social trend toward equal rights irrespective of race, ethnicity, or gender.

This phenomenon was associated with a rush toward nuclear family living the like of which had rarely been known. A grateful and well-meaning federal government saw to it that the G.I. Bill helped an entire generation of young ex-soldiers finance their years of higher education. The college years permitted them to segue into the more demanding, higher-paying jobs that the burgeoning economy was creating. The new money, and help from the government, made it possible for more families than ever to purchase a home and begin to realize the American dream. Suburbs pushed outward from around every urban center; entire planned cities were created where only farms had been before.

In the headlong rush of economic growth, liberal factions argued for and received expanded support for minority factions. By the 1950s and 1960s, the black community especially was being afforded much greater social opportunity, though the struggle would continue on into the current decade. Soon equal opportunity in all sectors of society was raising the wages of women and opening the way for activism overall. The generation which had struggled through the Great Depression was aging now, a population cohort living longer as a result of the wonders of modern medicine. To give the aged a well-deserved boost, a formerly little-noticed senior aid plan known as Social Security was widened into an ad hoc retirement program. In turn, it lead the way for federal backing of any number of other services. The phenomenal upheaval underway seemed about to produce what had never before seemed possible in human history, a social and economic transition in which inequality and hardship were no longer acceptable for anyone.

The economy was highly energized, as all the nation's interest groups struggled to obtain "fair rewards" for their members, but two critical factors were overlooked in the entitlement rush. First, no economy has ever maintained a constant growth trend without encountering plateaus. These come about either through external competition, such as the industrial emergence of Japan and Germany, or by rates of internal consumption overreaching investment, such as the gasoline shortages in the 1970s before the oil companies invested more in exploration in places such as Alaska. Second, entitlements are fine during times of rapid economic growth, but when the capacity to pay for them levels off or declines, while obligations continue unabated, the resulting financial imbalance can unleash any number of problems.

The few nay-sayers who saw what must one day come were ridiculed into silence at the time. Such talk was considered unpatriotic, for the philosophy of optimistic consumerism had taken hold in a major way. If problems developed at a future date, why, whoever was alive then could take care of them. For the moment everyone wanted to enjoy the boom times and blot out worries about the Cold War in a flurry of buying. And buy they did with unparalleled enthusiasm.

A generation passed in this way, and half of another. Then the big party slowed as the world changed.

Central to the concerns of America's post-Cold War existence is the question of what to do about taking care of our senior citizens. It is not merely that people now live well past the point where they can contribute as effectively as when they were younger. Emerging as part of the American Dream was the idea that elders simply ought to be able to live out their last years without having to work. Such a notion is unique to our time. In no other era was there wealth accumulated sufficient to even suggest it.

But from where should the money come? And how much? These questions are what this book is all about: How can we provide a pension system for our elders that is not based upon go-go economic pipe dreams, but rather firmly rooted in a solid cash-flow reality?

✯   ✯   ✯

Visualize the rise of net worth in the United States over the last half century as a pristine, white sandy beach, as we find ourselves standing at the shoreline, enjoying the benefits of the day. Our economy is growing, but much less dynamically than a couple of decades back. Little did we realize that the tide has been going out since 1983, when the Social Security tax rates were raised to their current levels. Now think of the outflow of money needed to pay elderly participants in state or federal pension plans and in Social Security, a portion of our nation's total net worth, as the current distance between the shoreline and the actual water's edge, at the low tide mark. As the tide begins to turn, the waves thunder and roar, growing larger, far larger than normal as it nears the beach, quickly covering up to the high tide mark, and threatening to go far beyond as unforeseen storms (the baby boomer generation and the boom-let caused by their children) gather strength many leagues out where the fertile trade winds mix with the moist, warm air of the ocean. Then these huge waves, rising up steeply, start taking up a greater and greater percentage of the white sandy beach, forcing us farther away from the once quiet shoreline, and into the quagmires of well-known hardships and disasters.

Can nature be changed? Could anyone have stopped the great hurricane of 1900 in Galveston? Not likely. But with planning, today Galveston, Texas, has sea-walls and rock-spines called jetties to break up incoming waves. *Planning was and is the key!*

The danger of a system strained to its limits was the situation that a few perceptive people noticed as long ago as the 1950s, first starting as a nagging suspicion to a significant minority during the 1970s, later to be confirmed in the 1980s, and now threatening us in the 1990s. Promised entitlements are on the verge of growing beyond our control. Something will have to change, and soon, or there will be no way to manage the payout. Default would put millions of elders at risk; raising workers' "income" by simply printing dollar bills would certainly make more Social Security money available, but the resulting inflation would damage the currency and probably wreck the economy; and raising Social Security taxes would siphon off cash needed for capital investment. It would be an understatement to say that none of these alternatives is attractive.

All great managed change is begun by a loud pronouncement. Someone dares to stand up and decry a folly or utter a call to action. In the present instance of the move to secure a financially sound retirement system for America's elders, the first attention-getting cry was made in 1982. The noted financial writer Andrew Tobias published a landmark essay in *Parade* magazine titled "How to Fix Social Security."

He laid out the facts as no politician could; common sense is rarely coincident with political resonance. Others had noticed several uncomfortable facts. By 1950, for the first fifteen years of the social program, there had been a 77 percent increase in Social Security benefit payments, but only a 0.5 percent increase in FICA taxes levied on income. FICA stands for Federal Insurance Contributions Act, which was the legislation authorizing Social Security taxes on wages of employed persons. This act provided for retirement and survivors and disability insurance. By 1970, other increases in allocated payments to retirees had risen by over 70 percent, yet a mere 3.2 percent increase was programmed into FICA receipts. At the turn of the 1980s, after a generation of declining family sizes, but ever-lengthening life spans, the ratio of workers who pay into the system to retirees had declined from 16.5 (workers) to 1 (recipient) down to approximately 3.2 to 1! The figures were incontrovertible.

There was absolutely no way that the rising tide of retirees could expect anything close to the anticipated retirement incomes based on increases enjoyed over the past sixty years. The original 1936 Social Security brochure simply stated, "From the time you are sixty-five years old, or more, and stop working, you will get a government check every month of your life, if you have worked." What is paid into Social Security is not put aside or invested for us. It goes to pay off current obligations. Without the necessary future proportion of paying younger persons to retired older persons, Tobias warned, the whole system must come crashing down, and soon.

The writing was so blunt that it caught everyone's attention, from the most reactionary pessimist to the most raving futurist. Millions of blanching readers stared down at the essay, absorbed the message, and felt sick to their stomachs. But this was America, the richest country on earth. Surely something could be done before disaster threatened to strike. Surely the situation wasn't hopeless?

Tobias had some plain-sighted suggestions, none of which was delightful, particularly for the politicians and older citizens. His general position was simple: in order to balance the money owed with the income generated the Social Security Administration must either take in more money or cut the growth of benefits.

More taxes? Cut those hard-won benefits? After two decades of severe inflation, aggravated by oil crises, Vietnam, and rampaging interest rates, the nation's collective blood pressure soared.

Well, if you didn't like that idea, what about taxing Social Security benefits? Or raising the mandatory retirement age from sixty-five to seventy? How about suspending automatic cost-of-living adjustments (COLAs) for a year or so, to give the system some breathing room?

Tobias concluded his little breath-stopper of an essay with the aphorism, as ominous in its understatement as it was ironic, that by putting Social Security back on "firm ground" it would signal to the financial markets of the world that ours was a country that could cope with its own future. In other words, we were in one heck of a fix. It was time to clean up our act or take the consequences.

A baker's dozen of years later, that's exactly what we are about to do. The Tobias alert produced a flurry of political rushing about and wringing of hands but little else. Except for Congress putting a small tax on benefits, nothing Tobias proposed has made it past the lobbyists or the political Old Guard.

Nevertheless, because it was too loud a remark to daydream past, Tobias's essay did get a lethargic hiccup from the Reagan administration. With the blessings of Congress, Reagan formed the National Commission on Social Security Reform (NCSSR), in the early eighties, to study the Social Security conundrum and see what could be done before the system went broke. When in doubt, form a committee. The NCSSR was comprised of eight Republicans and seven Democrats, a plethora of legislators and prominent business figures, all experts in using the time-perfected dodges that committees afford. Work seemed to be going on, but actually the whole process was nothing but smoke and mirrors. As they ducked and dodged, there was much trumpeting among NCSSR members about "their professional ethics and responsibilities" and "their obligations and charges" and "the mandate of history."

After full and timely consideration of their responsibility to keep constituents happy (and ignorant), their obligation to hold onto personal good image, their mandate to pass the buck, the members of the distinguished panel brushed past the important and chewed over the banal. Predictably, no one was up for confronting the truth, namely, that Social Security had gradually evolved from a New Deal add-on help notion for older people into a colossal, nearly mindless retirement system. The NCSSR hemmed and hawed over "entitlement ethics," "fair disbursements," and the firm recognition that *something must be done.*

Finally, rather than risk taking a hiding from vested interest groups, the NCSSR took the only alternative possible. It pontificated that when governments generate a bigger bill, more taxes must be raised to cover the cost. Perhaps new federal employees and non-profit organizations should no longer be exempted from paying Social Security tax (FICA)?

But don't jump to any fast conclusions. After all their deliberations, the members of the NCSSR wrote up a proposal, adjourned, and everyone went off to play golf.

The whole thing was a cynic's aphrodisiac. As the NCSSR dithered and shook its fists, one of its few nondelusional members, the despairing Congressman Bill Archer (R-Texas), sent a letter to one of his constituents about what was coming up. "I would hope," he wrote, "that the new National Social Security Commission will consider a complete revamping of Social Security, but, based on past actions, I cannot be optimistic." Realism was another matter. "While philosophically I would like to see a voluntary Social Security program, I have become convinced in recent years that this is just not going to happen and we must pursue reform of Social Security." Years later, the reform is still waiting to happen.

The conventional, nondisruptive wisdom was that if we didn't want Social Security to collapse under its own weight, with all the attending catastrophes that would produce, we must increase revenue, thereby depriving ourselves of much needed capital for investment. Congressman Archer remarked that, "any system must be fair to all generations, and this proposal is only a temporary fix, good for the short term." Bluntly put, Andrew Tobias would no doubt have referred to this as the use of a band-aid to stem a hemorrhage.

When Congress followed the NCSSR's suggestions, observers noticed that the new income seemed to have caused a surplus in the Social Security Trust Funds. Great! The wolf had been hit from a well-placed shot from the politicians' beebee gun and was no longer howling at the door. Whereupon a lot of people once more went to sleep on the subject of Social Security. Out of sight, out of mind. The exciting 1980s had plenty of matters to think about instead, including the tottering and stumbling expiration of European Communism. Unfortunately the wolf hadn't left. It was out there in the shadows, watching. Watching a multitrillion-dollar black hole grow ever more ominous inside the Social Security Trust Funds. Let me explain.

The financial pabulum purveyors in Congress have patronizingly opined that Social Security is okay. How do they know? Why, just look at the funds, they say. At the turn of 1994 it had a $384 billion surplus. Using a little simple algebra, at its rate of increase the surplus will reach $594 billion in fiscal 1996. Let's see, here; that would mean that by the year 2023 the surplus will reach no less than $5.6 trillion. Numbers don't lie! Look at all that cash. There's no problem with Social Security. Now get on out of here and let's get back to legislating.

Who do the politicians think they were kidding? Here's the heart-stopping truth.

If those figures actually represented real money, all *would* be well. But they don't. The surplus is tied up in government IOUs called special nonnegotiable bonds, redeemable only by the Treasury. The federal government has been trading out this paper in order to pay the normal expenses of running things. What's in the funds is the federal government's promise to pay, redeemable when the bonds reach their terms.

Can it, will it make good on its debts? Consider this.

Right now, the national debt is over $5 trillion. Using a little more simple algebra, we can calculate that it will pass $6 trillion after the turn of the twenty-first century, according to current government estimates. Let's be optimistic and hope that current efforts to stabilize the debt's growth will work by then. Hmmm. What was that about the government having paper instead of money in the Social Security Trust Funds? So . . . by 2025 according to the 1995 Trustees Report, Table lll.B3, the Trust Funds in current dollars will be $10.68 trillion, and that makes the real national debt around $16 trillion! It will take another economic lift-off the size of the post

World War II boom to cover all this debt. And that's just not going to happen.

Early in 1983, Congressman Bill Archer made brief headlines when he announced that the Social Security bail-out was no real solution. His real zinger followed. Instead of Social Security being used as a welfare agency, paying out money to recipients who had paid in only a fraction of what they were getting back, why not create a real, sensible pay-in, pay-out formula? People would get back what they put up in in the first place. What could be fairer than that?

The uproar and shouting that ensued, principally from the ranks of the gray-haired, was formidable indeed. The Democratic Old Guard whose members were running things on Capitol Hill at the time could see all their voters going south if they echoed this call. Instead, they heeded the NCSSR committee members' wisdom and kept their collective mouths shut, so virulent was the hoohaw.

Cut back the payout? That was ridiculous. Think of what it meant after inflation was factored in. Hardly anyone past the age of sixty-five would have enough money to pay the rent, or buy much more than day-old bread and co-op vegetables. Nobody could afford to go on cruises, or take trips to see the grandchildren. What was Archer thinking of?

Therein lies the rub. Just too much debt is coming up for the level of Social Security spending to keep on as it has, but all too few are willing to acknowledge, much less confront, the problem. They weren't thinking of the good of the system: they were concerned about their own political hides!

In one sense, Social Security has been a wonderful device for social engineering. It truly legitimized corporate aid for the elderly, thereby smoothing out the wrinkles in the traditional system in which families took care of their old folks as well as they could. That was good. There are too many citizens sleeping in the streets right now, without adding in the unfortunate or those without foresight who couldn't or just didn't save up anything for old age, and aren't tight with their offspring.

Looking at it another way, though, back in the days before families were spread throughout the country, older people were on a "pay-as-you-go" system that didn't take financial planning. It just happened. The idea of getting a boost of cash from the state or your former corporation, perhaps to spend on support but perhaps also just to blow self-indulgently, was not an issue. It just wasn't there. No one minded what they didn't know about, everybody got along the best they could.

History has altered matters, as it always does. Now family support of elders is accepted and we have to pay for it. That is a given. But how? Not the way we're doing it now; that's also a given.

The answer lies within the problem.

2

The Monster Grows
While Congress Dithers

"I am not an advocate for frequent changes in laws and Constitutions. But laws and institutions must go hand in hand with the progress of the human mind. We might as well require a man to wear still the coat which fitted him when a boy as civilized society to remain ever under the regimen of their barbarous ancestors."

Thomas Jefferson, 1816

These are very strong and very forthright words from one of our Founding Fathers and yet this simple and straightforward thought of Thomas Jefferson, voiced over one hundred and seventy years ago, namely, "Institutions must advance also to keep pace with the times," is as true today as it was when first spoken. It's as though Jefferson was talking about the Social Security system.

When President Franklin Roosevelt started Social Security in 1935 during the depths of the Great Depression, he gave the working people of this country something they had never had before, a helping hand in their retirement years. This was done by promising a modest government check for the balance of their lives, if they had paid into the system during their working years. Social Security was never meant to be more than that, and it stayed that way until the early fifties.

It was during this period that militant and "let's-get-ours" attitudes began to develop throughout the country. It was as though these groups found the mother lode, just as the hardy pioneers did when they struck pay dirt during the Gold Rush days of 1849 in California, and then the race was on. Groups of people such as the elderly began to realize that by banding together under a number of different banners, they could make demands on the congressional money machine as they had never before and get the short-term results they wanted, such as increased monthly benefits.

Little thought was given to paying for these benefit increases, which were so generously bestowed during the sixties and the seventies. The Old Guard Democrats in Congress simply told their constituents as well as the rest of the country there was nothing to worry about. But everyone knew that their sons and daughters and their grandsons and granddaughters would pick up the tab in the long run.

Unions saw how successful this approach was and took their demands for higher wages and benefits to new heights with little regard for the future and what it would do to the profitability of these private-sector businesses. The airline saga is a good example of the results of this thinking. The demise of Eastern Airlines and Pan American World Airways was tragic; these closures hastened the senseless end of a historic era, not to mention the thousands of jobs that were lost. A double-edged sword cuts both ways.

It was at this time that the Democrat-controlled Congress then realized that Social Security could lead to another great possibility. Keep the elderly happy with steady increases in benefits and their political future was safe, as the elderly could be depended upon to vote, and in large numbers. Congressmen and women smiled as they became content, happy, and *reelected.* What could be better? The day of reckoning, that was something to think about later. These legislators failed to realize where this path would lead them. During the forty years that the Democrats controlled Congress the government grew as never before. In addition to expanding Social Security, other government programs to help everyone and everything from the arts to the needy sprang up. The money machine was working overtime. The national debt grew by leaps and bounds until in 1994 it stood at over $4 trillion. To hide this gruesome fact those inside the beltway started talking about fiscal deficits. This was an interesting ploy by those in power to only tell what was going on in the current fiscal year while ignoring completely the ballooning national debt.

As an example they were happy to tell the American people that the deficit was reduced $100 billion last year because it went from $250 billion to $150 billion. In reality they had increased the already burgeoning debt another $150 billion. The rate of increase had been slowed to be sure, but the total national debt kept rising.

The American people finally began to realize that the money machine could not go on forever. Even deep pockets become empty, and in the case of Congressional spending those pockets have been yours and mine. Fortuitously 1994 brought an end to this pie-in-the-sky thinking. The voters said they wanted no more thoughtless and ill-considered legislation. They want a sensible government with sound priorities. There were too many programs that had mushroomed far beyond all sane expectations.

And this same thinking holds true for the largest people-benefit program the government has. This institution called Social Security, as it is now structured, has just about outlived its day. Congress and the various administrations over the past fifteen years have borrowed over $500 billion and have no way of paying it back, without digging deep into your pocket and mine. The Social Security tax, or FICA withholding as it is also called, the foundation of this program, has reached the point where any further increases would make it a very regressive tax. How will average workers feel when they see that Social Security taxes and income taxes together will take a 30 percent bite out of their weekly paycheck? Many people argue that a new concept is needed to bring this monster under control and to serve the working men and women of this country into and beyond the twenty-first century. Congress just did not learn the financial lessons of the fifties and sixties, when it continually raised benefits without increasing the FICA taxes to handle the increase.

Even though Congress staggered through the eighties and kept the system going with huge increases in Social Security taxes, lawmakers really had no idea how long it would last. They set the rates high enough to generate huge surpluses for the next two or three decades. Not being happy with that, they proceeded to borrow from it and spend in other areas.

Congress did this in a way that shows a genius for working the system so its hands would be clean while it could continue to say that it was only doing what the law requires. But who made the laws? The law Congress enacted said that any surplus funds from Social Security collections must be invested in government bonds. Not just any bonds a brokerage could buy, but in a special class of bonds only redeemable by the Treasury with the blessing of Congress. Now in the nineties, with a huge deficit in the system and the baby boomers close to retirement, Congress has no answer.

Now these IOUs (these so-called special bonds) have taken up so much of the Social Security Trust Funds that Congress will shortly be right back where it started in 1982. Only now there will be a gigantic debt load (in the trillions), 80 million baby boomers who will be reaching retirement age, and costs that will take some real work to bring under control. This is Congress at its finest!

If the lawmakers had taken the surplus each year and invested it in actual profit-making vehicles, rather than camouflaging the national debt, they would now have a large enough surplus to take care of the baby boomer generation upon retirement. These surpluses would now be making billions of dollars each year in interest alone.

What *do* we have? We have over $400 billion in IOUs that no one can redeem except the U.S. Treasury. There are advocates who think this is just fine. They point out that in 1993 these special bonds earned 8.5 percent interest. Fine, but where is Congress going to get the money to pay this interest, that is if it ever plans to actually pay the interest? There is only one place and we all know it. It's from you and me. These advocates are serious and well intentioned. They believe that bigger government will always be the answer. They just cannot believe otherwise. The withdrawal from this belief would be just too much for them.

The truth is there is only one way to see to the needs of a growing elderly population without wreaking havoc with every other entitlement program—increase taxes. But that is no longer a valid answer. If taxes should ever increase substantially to meet the need, voters would be in a furor. The value of these special bonds will be close to a trillion dollars at the turn of the century, and in today's or even tomorrow's dollars, that is a lot of money.

What it all boils down to is: the average working man and woman will be paying for their retirement twice, or maybe even three times, first through the normal paycheck withholding and again through increased taxes and an increased national debt. It could also be done by increasing the Social Security tax withheld from the current 6.2 percent of a worker's gross pay to 12.4 percent. No one in Congress has had the will to tell America's working people what's in store for them in the future.

Hundreds of years ago we built lighthouses to aid in navigation. Why? They directed ships away from the pitfalls and shoals. No sane skipper of any vessel would steer his ship directly into the light. His common sense and expertise would prevail.

Can the same be said of Congress? In retrospect there have been any number of signals and warnings about the ever growing Social Security problems. If our leaders on Capitol Hill simply continue the same, shortsighted, "hope-we-can-get-away-with-this" thinking, the Social Security ship will be on the rocks of desperation. Then any solution decided upon will be very painful to everyone.

In 1995 there are many newspapers, writers, and economists warning of what is to come. There is even a growing number of legislators in Congress sounding warnings. The Republican leadership in both the House and the Senate has an opportunity to show its stuff. The Democrats took forty years to show that they didn't have what it takes, but the Republicans will not be so lucky.

The people of this country are fed up. If a congressman were to hold a town meeting in his or her district and simply listen to his constituents, perhaps some light would go on and bells would ring as to what the people really want. Then that member of Congress could go back to Washington, compare notes with colleagues, and things might really begin to happen.

The Bipartisan Commission on Entitlement and Tax Reform of 1994 under Senator Bob Kerrey (D-Neb.) has gone the way of the National Commission for Social Security Reform of 1982. In fact the commission actually did less except to further warn the country and keep the story alive. No one can say they haven't been fully warned.

In the early eighties many writers expounded on Social Security's problems and even came up with some good ideas, but no one inside the beltway took them seriously, or if they did, nothing was done about it. As an example, in July 1982, the *Houston Chronicle* ran a story, headlined:

"SOCIAL SECURITY TO BORROW $7 BILLION"

This major news event told of a startling announcement by then Social Security Commissioner John Svahn, that the Social Security System must borrow, for the first time in its history, $7 billion to meet its obligations. He said that changes will have to be made in the system this year (1982) or next. Social Security taxes may have to be raised as much as 25 percent to maintain the present benefits. Then former commissioner Svahn expounded on what everyone else was thinking. There were only two options: increase withholding rates or the current recipients receive less. The current recipients are for the most part your parents and grandparents. The options looked grim.

Svahn said the worst problem facing the system is that 70 percent of the American people don't believe that Social Security will be around when they get ready to retire in the next two or three decades. Then Svahn further claimed that in the year 2015 the Social Security Trust Funds will need $1.5 trillion to keep up today's benefit structure.

This story should have chilled every working American to the bone, but the politicians did their usual great job of lulling everyone back to sleep with rhetoric about Social Security being in fine shape and that it will have a surplus until the year 2039.

Things have changed very little in the past decade. Just recently in a statement right out of the October 4, 1994 hearing on Social Security, Robert Lukefahr, co-founder of the Third Millennium, a group of concerned young Americans from ages twenty-five to thirty-five, spoke of a survey that showed 67 percent of young people do not believe Social Security will even exist by the time they retire. In addition, 83 percent of young people believe the government has made promises it cannot keep, and 87 percent do not think the Social Security System will have the money available to provide them benefits when they retire.

Texas Republican Congressman Bill Archer, then ranking minority member and now the 1995 chairman of the powerful House Ways and Means Committee, said in a *Houston Chronicle* story, "We had a wonderful opportunity to do something about Social Security when President Reagan set up the National Commission on Social Security Reform (NCSSR) in 1982, but it was frittered away."

The reason this happened is that many congressional members of the commission could not see beyond the next election. Instead of really trying to do something that would help the working people of this country, most of the members worried about how they would look back home. So they just raised taxes. This pushed the problem on into the nineties. In doing so they actually did solve the problem, but they didn't realize it. More on this in Part Three.

If we fail to do anything about Social Security and retirement systems within the next few years, these systems will become top-heavy with too many recipients being supported by too few workers. The systems themselves will then force many difficult changes on all of us.

Many times over the past decade it has been said by writers and columnists that everyone is for reform but no one is willing to stand up and be counted. All of these good intentions mean very little. The problem seems to be that no one has the right way to pay for Social Security without causing a great deal of consternation to one group or another. A second reason is that the actual problem will not be acute for another decade, and by then most of today's lawmakers will no longer be around.

Today the younger generation is beginning to realize that under the current system they are paying more and more, with a good chance of receiving a lot less than today's recipients. They may never get back in benefits what they put into the system during their working life. That is why we need a completely new concept to bring Social Security into the new century. Make no mistake about it, the Social Security Revolution has started!

Our first revolution started in many places throughout the thirteen colonies. It started in the beautiful, tree-covered towns of Lexington and Concord, then on to the industrial cities of Boston and New York, and on to the lovely southern city of Charleston, just to name a few.

It took a number of years to get everyone together with one idea, that was eventually put into writing in Philadelphia. But once it was given form in the Declaration of Independence events moved fast.

Our Founding Fathers from Georgia to Massachusetts got together in Philadelphia and pledged their allegiance and lives to something greater than themselves, and George Washington took them through many trying times until the British surrender at Yorktown, Virginia.

In much the same way, many different groups and individuals continue to write and speak about new ways to bring Social Security into the coming century, exploring methods that will not heap a greater load onto the already overburdened taxpayers of this country.

The retirees of today have earned their retirement. In the past sixty years they have suffered through a Great Depression and the Dust Bowl of the western plains and fought through a number of wars (World War II, Korea, the Cold War, and even Vietnam) while helping to build this country to where it is today. They have paid their dues.

At the same time we must all look to the future. The young people of today *are* the future. Today's youth are just like the young people of all generations; they rarely think about retirement until after they reach middle age. It's the natural order of things. Middle age has that effect on people. Yet the early working years, ages twenty to forty, make all the difference in what their future retirement will look like.

The Social Security tax that everyone pays today is something everyone takes for granted. It's a given. That is the key, the cornerstone for turning this Social Security problem around. No one realizes, especially the younger generation, that the $20 to $50 per week taken out of their pay and properly invested can wind up being a huge retirement fund when that time rolls around. To do this is simplicity itself. Chapter 18 fully explains how this can be done. To the average working person there will be no change at all, except that every year they will receive a statement showing just how much has accumulated on their behalf.

The average person doesn't realize that over $200 billion in Social Security taxes (FICA) is taken out, in total, from all paychecks each year. This will continue to increase annually and by the turn of the century it will be close to $300 billion. This is the money that everyone in the government says is being invested for your retirement. Private sector employers also feel this same sting as they are mandated to put up matching funds.

By the year 2002 the actual funds taken in by the U.S. Treasury will almost match the outlay. The surpluses Social Security will show after this period will all be paper transactions. A good example of this is the way the government handles withholding from the military. The U.S. Treasury withholds the 6.2 percent from a soldier's pay and then just sends an IOU over to the Social Security Trust Funds. Talk about creative bookkeeping and arm's length transactions, the people who run the U.S. Treasury must really take some special courses to keep everything straight.

It is truly tragic that Congress is so narrow-minded and short-sighted that it can see in only one direction. It must be admitted, though, that pressures from many different groups can warp a person's thinking and make it very hard to see other solutions.

The current solution of big government continues to be the only answer to the Social Security problem, or so lawmakers want us all to believe. Yet at the same time Congress has shown in a very quiet way that there is another safe, sound, and prosperous answer to this retirement problem. Ask any government employee under the Federal Employees Retirement System (FERS) what the TSP is! Or better still, look for the answer in chapter 11. You won't believe it.

If Congress had just taken the simple step of leaving the Social Security Trust Funds alone—if it hadn't borrowed from them—the problems that are looming on the horizon would not come into play for another fifty years. The 1994 Trustees Report for Social Security shows that the surpluses that have accumulated over the past decade would now be earning over $36 billion a year in interest and dividends had they been invested in secure, low-risk investments. That would be real income and not just U.S. Treasury IOUs. The key words here are "real income and IOUs." One enhances growth and the other retards it. The choice should be clear, except perhaps inside the beltway.

The monster has grown to an unmanageable size, not because of the system itself, but because of those running it. Temporary solutions never work because a day of reckoning always comes. In less than ten years Social Security will no longer have an actual surplus at the end of the year. Then what will Congress do? All it will have is the paper interest the government has been charging itself. At that time no amount of creative bookkeeping will get the job done.

On a par with this type of thinking is what Congress does with the national debt. These days Congress keeps telling the American people the deficit is going down each year and yet the national debt keeps going up each year! Ask your congressman to explain that one to you.

The days of an honest accounting from those inside the beltway may soon be upon us.

Reflect on these words uttered by John Adams in 1818:

The Revolution was affected before the war commenced. The Revolution was in the minds and hearts of the people. This radical change in the principles, opinions, sediments and affections of the people was the real American Revolution.

3

What Franklin Roosevelt
Really Wanted

"We do not believe that men exist merely to strengthen the state or be cogs in an economic machine. We do believe that governments are created to serve the people."

Harry S. Truman, 1948

And that is what President Truman's predecessor, Franklin D. Roosevelt, believed. Roosevelt was so convinced of it in fact that, when he took office in 1933, he developed a group of programs designed to help jump-start an economy that had taken a disastrous slide into a long and deep depression as a result of the wild, unchecked financial markets of the roaring twenties. This period of time in the early thirties is now known as the New Deal.

Before Franklin Roosevelt took office the stock market had crashed in 1929 and the Great Depression was well underway. To compound the crisis in the financial markets there had been several years of very little rain throughout the farm belt of Oklahoma,

Kansas, and Nebraska. This prolonged period of drought saw the destruction of large areas of land as the parched soil was whipped into large clouds of dust. This area of the country soon became renowned as the Dust Bowl. The result was many foreclosures of countless farms and the exodus of families to areas of the country where they hoped to make a fresh start. One of President Roosevelt's most famous remarks during this period was "The only thing we have to fear is fear itself," a phrase from one of his notable fireside chats in which he sought to ease the tensions of the time and reassure anxious citizens that the government would help them through these tough times.

As soon as President Roosevelt took office he and a group of unofficial advisors started in a new direction, and during the now famous First Hundred Days of his administration FDR started putting the New Deal into practice.

During these first days, Congress passed a number of Roosevelt's important programs, many of which are still with us today. The programs enacted into law included the creation of the Federal Deposit Insurance Corporation (FDIC) to protect the savings of bank patrons; the Securities and Exchange Commission (SEC), which provides rules and regulations for investing; the Civilian Conservation Corps (CCC), which has long since been phased out but served a very useful purpose as a source for public works projects; and the Tennessee Valley Authority (TVA), which for many decades developed a system of dams and hydroelectric power projects.

During President Roosevelt's second hundred days in 1935 a number of important measures were passed by Congress. To the thinking of the elderly and eventually all working men and women, the high point was the passage of the Social Security Act.

Social Security was conceived by Roosevelt and his economic advisors in order to supplement the incomes of those who were elderly and in desperate need during the Great Depression. It was one of the pump-priming economic ideas, mixed in with notions of social fairness, at a time when such thoughts were seldom discussed. It was aimed at the poor and middle class who needed the help.

FDR knew there was strong opposition as many thought it would lead to socialism. But with the election of a large Democratic majority in the mid-term elections of 1934, he gained the muscle needed to get the job done and pressed forward. In August 1935, Roosevelt signed into law the Social Security Act to cover the workers and senior citizens.

To put it simply, Roosevelt wanted a modicum of security for those who had worked and struggled all their lives in honest toil. These were the folks who had raised their families, had gone to war in the service of their country, and never found a way of putting aside a nest egg for their elder years. His thoughts were not of others who had the wherewithal to insure their own tranquillity in later years. Rather, his thoughts were with the hard-working fishermen, the workers in the factories and mills, and the everyday Janes and Joes who are the foundation of this country.

There were many who thought that Social Security Act would not pass constitutional muster, but in 1938 the U.S. Supreme Court upheld the act, and the rest is history.

There have been countless books written about FDR and Social Security, but nothing expresses President Roosevelt's thinking about this innovative program better than the original brochure given to all workers in the late 1930s. This act was embodied in a simple four-page document that said it all quite clearly, without all of today's legalese.

This Social Security Act may not be as well known as many other great documents, but it should be since it now effects the lives and futures of over 135 million American workers, as well as 42 million retired workers. What follows is the entire four-page brochure given to all working people of 1936. Reproduced verbatim from the original, this document shows the exact style and prose of the 1930s.

To refresh your memories, in 1940 a good starting wage was thirty-five cents per hour and most people worked six days a week.

A family of five could live on $30 a week. An apartment rented for $35 per month and a car could be bought for $150. The maximum you paid for the first three years was $30 per year; it wasn't until 1959 that workers paid over $100 per year as a maximum.

SECURITY IN YOUR OLD AGE

Social Security Board
Washington, D.C.

To Employees of Industrial and Business Establishments

FACTORIES—SHOPS—MINES—MILLS—STORES OFFICES AND OTHER PLACES OF BUSINESS

*   *   *

Beginning November 24, l936, the United States Government will set up a Social Security account for you, if you are eligible. To understand your obligations, rights, and benefits you should read the following general explanation.

There is now a law in this country which will give about 26 million working people something to live on when they are old and have stopped working. This law, which gives other benefits, too, was passed last year by Congress and is called the Social Security Act.

Under this law the United States Government will send checks every month to retired workers, both men and women, after they have passed their 65th birthday, and have met a few simple requirements of the law.

WHAT THIS MEANS TO YOU

This means that if you work in some factory, shop, mine, mill, store, office, or almost any other kind of business or industry, you will be earning benefits that will come to you later on. From the time you are 65 years old, or more, and stop working, you will get a Government check every month of your life, if you have worked some time (one day or more) in each of any 5 years after 1936, and have earned during that time a total of $2,000 or more.

The checks will come to you as a right. You will get them regardless of the amount of property or income you may have. They are what the law calls "Old-Age Benefits" under the Social Security Act. If you prefer to keep working after you are 65, the monthly checks from the Government will begin coming to you whenever you decide to retire.

The Amount of Your Checks

How much you will get when you are 65 years old will depend entirely on how much you earn in wages from your industrial or business employment between January 1, 1937, and your 65th birthday. A man or woman who gets good wages and has a steady job most of his or her life can get as much as $85 a month for life after age 65. The least you can get in monthly benefits, if you come under the law at all, is $10 a month.

IF YOU ARE NOW YOUNG

Suppose you are making $25 a week and are young enough now to go on working for 40 years. If you make an average of $25 a week for 52 weeks in each year, your check when you are 65 years old will be $53 a month for the rest of your life. If you make $50 a week, you will get $74.50 a month for the rest of your life after age 65.

IF YOU ARE NOW MIDDLE-AGED

But suppose you are about 55 years old and have 10 years to work before you are 65. Suppose you make only $15 a week on the average. When you stop work at age 65 you will get a check for $19 each month for the rest of your life. If you make $25 a week for 10 years, you will get a little over $23 a month from the Government as long as you live after your 65th birthday.

IF YOU SHOULD DIE BEFORE AGE 65

If you should die before you begin to get your monthly checks, your family will get a payment in cash, amounting to $3\frac{1}{2}$ cents on every dollar of wages you have earned after 1936. If, for example, you should die at age 64, and if you had earned $25 a week for 10 years before that time, your family would receive $455. On the other hand, if you have not worked enough to get the regular monthly checks by the time you are 65, you will get a lump sum, or if you should die your family or estate would get a lump sum. The amount of this, too, will be $3\frac{1}{2}$ cents on every dollar of wages you earn after 1936.

TAXES

The same law that provides these old-age benefits for you and other workers, sets up certain new taxes to be paid to the United States Government. These taxes are collected by the Bureau of Internal Revenue of the U.S. Treasury Department, and inquiries concerning them should be addressed to that bureau. The law also creates an "Old-Age Reserve Account" in the United States Treasury, and Congress is authorized to put into this reserve account each year enough money to provide for the monthly payments you and other workers are to receive when you are 65.

YOUR PART OF THE TAX

The taxes called for in this law will be paid both by your employer and by you. For the next 3 years you will pay maybe 15 cents a week, maybe 25 cents a week, maybe 30 cents or more, according to what you earn. This is to say, during the next 3 years, beginning January 1, 1937, you will pay 1 cent for every dollar you earn, and at the same time your employer will pay 1 cent for every dollar you earn, up to $3,000 a year. Twenty-six million other workers and their employers will be paying at the same time.

After the first 3 years—that is to say, beginning in 1940—you will pay, and your employer will pay, 1½ cents for each dollar you earn, up to $3,000 per year. This will be the tax for 3 years, and then, beginning in 1943, you will pay 2 cents, and so will your employer, for every dollar you earn for the next three years. After that, you and your employer will each pay half a cent more for 3 years, and finally, beginning in 1949, twelve years from now, you and your employer will each pay 3 cents on each dollar you earn, up to $3,000 a year. That is the most you will ever pay.

YOUR EMPLOYER'S PART OF THE TAX

The Government will collect both of these taxes from your employer. Your part of the tax will be taken out of your pay. The Government will collect from your employer an equal amount out of his own funds.

This will go on just the same if you go to work for another employer, so long as you work in a factory, shop, mine, mill, office, store, or other such place of business. (Wages earned in employment as farm workers, domestic workers in private homes, Government workers, and on a few other kinds of jobs are not subject to this tax.)

OLD-AGE RESERVE ACCOUNT

Meanwhile, the Old-Age Reserve fund in the United States Treasury is drawing interest, and the Government guarantees it will never earn less than 3 percent. This means that 3 cents will be added to every dollar in the fund each year.

Maybe your employer has an old-age pension plan for his employees. If so, the Government's old-age benefit plan will not have to interfere with that. The employer can fit his plan into the Government plan.

What you get from the Government plan will always be more than you have paid in taxes and usually more than you can get for yourself by putting away the same amount of money each week in some other way.

Note that the program exempts government workers from the Social Security tax. This is the basis for cities and counties to opt out of Social Security until Congress closed this option in 1984. The account of one such program can be found in chapter 15.

There are very few copies left and one of the original copies of this brochure is in the National Archives in Washington, D.C. This document was the start of a social program that has lasted over half a century. If you would like a copy of this Social Security document, contact your local congressperson. It has grown to the point where this program now has a profound effect on the government, the federal budget, the federal debt, the annual deficit, and all the working people of this country. It is hard to imagine what we would do without it.

The original Social Security plan put into practice in 1936 was simple. Each individual would pay part of his income into trust funds which would generate interest, repaying them a small trickle of income at retirement. The payers must put money in long enough to qualify. Eligibility requirements as well as monthly benefits are entirely in the hands of Congress, and can be changed even after a person has retired. In short, Social Security was not a retirement vehicle per se. It was a way to help low-income, poorly educated people to have a little bit of security when they became too old for vigorous work. It was never intended to help an executive of a large company, for instance, nor anyone with the funds to handle their own retirement.

President Roosevelt said this about Social Security. "We can never insure one hundred percent of the population against one hundred percent of the hazards and vicissitudes of life, but we have tried to frame a law which will give some measure of protection to the average citizen and his family against the loss of a job and against poverty-ridden old age."

This did not mean that the program should stay the same. It couldn't and it hasn't. Since Social Security's inception in 1935, Congress and the various administrations have made many changes. Unfortunately many of these changes have been questionable, but this patchwork job was done in order to deal with political issues, without wondering about the effects on the people as a whole.

And the political world of Capitol Hill is not the real world that some two hundred million Americans live and work in. Congress actually thought about Social Security very little, except when it could affect votes. Senators and representatives set up their own deluxe retirement system and a great retirement plan for all federal employees. Chapter 11 outlines the whole wonderful tale of federal retirement plans.

It was only after Congress found a need to raise more money that it looked upon government employees as an untapped source and went ahead in the early 1980s to include them in Social Security. Only in this way could FICA taxes be withheld.

Probably very few people realize that all those who work for the Social Security Administration to implement this Social Security program are federal government employees who do not depend upon

Social Security for their retirement. They receive a government pension which is normally two or three times better than any private pension plan, and many times better than Social Security.

It is time these Social Security administrators and Congress really try to understand that the people this system serves no longer believe in large part that the current system can survive or do the job intended under current circumstances.

While the original Social Security document outlines a simple plan of benefits, today the Social Security Administration spans thousands of pages and policies taking experts and lawyers to explain them. Even with all these pages the system is badly in need of repair. Why? Because Congress took a simple idea that President Roosevelt conceived and, over the years, turned it into a full-blown retirement system by continuing to give large increases every year. But the lawmakers neglected one thing: they didn't properly finance these increases.

Without realizing it, Congress, in 1983, put in place the necessary mechanisms to set up an entirely new system that would answer the needs of the twenty-first century. Whether it has the courage to put the people of the United States first, ahead of any political considerations, is another question. If it does we will have a win-win situation that will last a very long time. Congress did this in a most curious way. In 1983 to solve the bankruptcy problems that had faced Social Security for several years (from 1979 through 1983), legislators increased the Social Security tax rates high enough to create a surplus each year for approximately twenty-five years. If Congress had invested this surplus in profit-making vehicles, the country as well as the Social Security system would now be in great shape with an interest income of over $40 billion a year. In twenty-five years this would show a total in excess of $500 billion in interest alone, and the principal would still be intact.

Instead, Congress decided this was a pay-as-you-go system and took the surplus and used it as normal operating funds to pay regu-

lar bills. Today there is almost $485 billion in deficit IOUs in the So-
cial Security Trust Funds, and there are four trust funds. This means
there is a trillion dollar swing from a positive to a negative balance.)

But strangely enough the American worker did not lose from this
ill-advised process. By setting the rates as high as they did Congress
made the *spread* large enough to take care of the current retirees,
while at the same time it will enable the younger generations to pull
away from this antiquated system and set up a new one, without
penalty to anyone. By just rearranging the numbers the system becomes an immediate success!

Congress itself proved that privatization of Social Security is the
only way to prevent a future default of the system. Congressional action and inaction has shown time and again that politics and sound
retirement do not and will not mix.

> "The care of human life and happiness, and not their destruction,
> is the first and only legitimate object of good government."
>
> Thomas Jefferson, 1810

4

Social Security Today

"There is no cause half so sacred as the cause of a people. There is no idea so uplifting as the idea of service to humanity."

Woodrow Wilson, 1912

As humankind has progressed through the eons, many landmarks, or perhaps we should call them "guide posts," have been left to chronicle its progress.

In 1215, in Runneymede, England, the Magna Carta was signed by King John. He was forced to do so by nobles who could no longer tolerate his tyranny. The document recognized the right of the individual; it was a start toward democracy and the freedom of humankind. With it came the realization that all people should have a say in how they are governed. Years later, England's King Edward I acknowledged the rights granted under this Great Charter and acceded to the barons' wishes that established a new conception of taxation. From that point forward, never again would a king of England be able to legally impose a tax without the consent of Parliament.

In Philadelphia, on July 4, 1776, the Declaration of Independence was signed by representatives of thirteen colonies because the people of America were no longer willing to bow down to autocratic rule from England. The English, it seems, had forgotten why they had mounted a hard-fought struggle in their early days. Greed has a way of doing that to people, clouding their thinking. Short-term gain is never worth a possible long-term disaster.

Social Security had its beginnings in the earliest times through programs started by Judaism and early Christianity. The ancient Jews paid a tax for the benefit of the poor. This idea continued during the Middle Ages when knighthood and chivalry were at their height in Western Europe. Secular groups of the period founded charities, and ecclesiastical orders established monasteries, to take care of the sick and needy.

During the Industrial Revolution of the 1700s and the early 1800s, life began to change from a vast agricultural and rural society to a primarily industrial and urban one. During this period many farming families moved to the cities to work in factories, often at low wages and no benefits. These families suffered many hardships and privations, which eventually led to the development of social insurance in Europe and in America.

Recognizing this, in the late 1800s the Charity Organization Society started a professional group to help the needy on a full-time basis. It took up the challenge and served the less fortunate in England, the United States, and Canada. Then in 1898 this Charity Society founded the New York School of Philanthropy to train people for positions with social agencies. After years of service to the community, this school grew and became world renowned. It is now the New School of Social Research.

These private endeavors helped to wake up the federal government to the public's needs. By 1925 the federal government opened its eyes and began to recognize that there were many risks facing the work force in an increasingly industrialized nation. This led to the development of a number of social insurance programs to handle many problems such as injury on the job, disability, unemployment, and old age. By 1929 all but four states had laws covering workers' compensation for injury or those killed while working.

The severe depression of the 1930s brought home the reality that most American workers were dependent on factors beyond their individual control for economic security and retirement.

As industry grew and spread throughout many parts of the country, the government realized that federal action was necessary. Private organized charities did not, at the time, have the financial resources to cope with the growing needs of the people hardest hit. That is one reason why in 1932 the federal government started programs of direct relief.

Warehouses were set up throughout the country where folks without food or work could get such staples as flour, beans, and rice. This program helped many families through the depression years. These warehouses conjure up many memories for the elders of today. The memory of one such elder is that of a young boy of eight walking down to the big brown warehouse with his mother, his little red wagon in tow, to receive the basic necessities. A realization that did not occur to him until many years later.

President Roosevelt was to the people of that era a man for all seasons. He brought them through the tough economic times and left a legacy for this generation in the form of Social Security. Can there be any doubt why elders tend to think highly and are very protective of this program? The symbolism is as much a part of it as the actual financial help.

A helping hand was the president's intention, but through the past five decades the growth of the country, the advances in technology, and the population explosion have expanded the Social Security system like an exploding star. Centrifugal force took over and the system mushroomed out in all directions. President Johnson's Great Society continued this rapid and unchecked growth of all social welfare programs, which included Social Security. Inertia fueled the momentum as one Democratic-controlled Congress after another, feeling this surge that was unleashed, and, realizing this was the way to continued reelection, swept to new heights of fiscal irresponsibility. Senators and congresspersons continually raised and expanded the benefits without any real thought of the consequences. Social Security was well on its way to disaster, for it was virtually out of control.

But we are getting ahead of ourselves. Let's continue the story from the forties.

Social Security was put into place at the end of a deeply troubled era in American history, and before the start of World War II, which ushered in the high-tech era of the forties and beyond. It gave the elderly a basis for hope and a framework on which to build in the future. All things great seem to have a troubled or uncertain start, and Social Security, along with efforts to insure a decent retirement, was no different.

Title II of the Act created an Old Age Reserve Account and authorized payments to those over age sixty-five who had worked and made contributions through payroll withholding. This withholding came to be known as FICA taxes. The maximum benefit an individual could receive was $85 per month, until Congress adjusted this in the fifties. In 1940, the first monthly check for $22.54 was paid to Ida Mae Fuller of Ludlow, Vermont. Over the past six decades these benefits have been adjusted until today the maximum payment is $1,248 per month. Today, in 1995, more than 150 million individuals are engaged in work covered by Social Security and some 42.2 million retirees are now receiving cash benefits each month.

With the outbreak of World War II our society and the country as a whole changed in dramatic fashion. Everyone had been geared up as a result of the war and there was no going back. Everything and everyone was trying to catch up.

And so it was with the elderly. One problem with the way Social Security worked out is that the tiny amount of benefits, based on actual individual investment, didn't amount to much. After World War II ended, prices stayed high but Social Security benefits lagged far behind. Liberal groups began to clamor for a bigger pay-out for those not enjoying the mainstream benefits of a burgeoning American economy, such as welfare payments, and equal pay for equal work for both women and minorities. As services for other groups enlarged at taxpayer expense, Social Security recipients began to receive more than their initial inputs should have allowed. In a wildly growing economic time, who cared? The country's generosity seemed limitless and would last forever. After all, weren't we the greatest country in the world!

That was then, this is now. In 1950 the ratio of taxpayers to Social Security recipients was a strong 16.5 taxpayers to 1 recipient, and the average number of years a retiree received benefits was seven. In 1995 the ratio is approaching 3.2 to 1, while the number of years that a retiree receives benefits has skyrocketed to fifteen. In addition, Social Security has had a number of benefit programs attached on to it over the past two generations, such as the disability feature and the death benefits, both added in 1939, which have continued to grow with the increased population, all of which have to be paid for somehow. Right now we are paying far more than was ever intended to people who are living longer than ever before. To compound the problem the elders are also expecting essentially unlimited Medicare help in their declining years.

As of August 1994, Social Security once again become an independent agency. It ceased being part of the sprawling bureaucracy of the Department of Health and Human Services. You'll recall that when it was first established some sixty years ago it was an independent agency called the Social Security Board.

The intervening period has witnessed six decades of unplanned growth of benefits given by lawmakers who thought very little about where the money was coming from. It's as though we planted a tree and then let it grow, not caring how tall, wide or misshapen it became. Instead of pruning and caring for the tree, we simply let it grow, sprouting branches everywhere. Then as time went by natural forces wore the tree down until it was in sad shape and long past the point that anything could be done to keep it looking like the beautiful tree it once was.

Before we go any further, let's take a look at some interesting statistics outlining what Social Security has been doing over the years. These figures come from the 1994 Trustees Report for Social Security and from Congressional Research Reports.

As of 1994 there were 42.2 million recipients (that is people receiving Social Security benefits). California and Florida together have over 7 million of these folks. There are 137.8 million taxpayers supporting these 42.2 million retirees. In 1940 the average wage earner paid $12 per year into FICA (Social Security taxes); in 1993 the average worker paid $5,529 as a maximum. In fifty-three years the Social Security tax increased over 460 times, and it's still going up in the coming years. On the benefits side, recipient Ida Mae Fuller received $22.54 per month in 1940. In 1995 the maximum that a recipient can be paid is $1,248 per month. That's an increase of fifty-two times over the original pay out.

The figures for monies paid in are bigger than those paid out. In fact, the amount paid in is nine times larger. If payout was 460 times larger than the original amount—equal to the amount of increase in Social Security taxes over the years—today a recipient should be getting $10,120 per month. Now that's a retirement to look forward to.

It is easy to understand why seniors are worried about anyone who wants to change Social Security. To more than 60 percent of the current recipients Social Security is their major source of income and support. Second, for the most part their income-producing days are over and they have no where else to turn.

The Entitlements Commission of 1994, chaired by Senator Bob

Kerrey (D-Neb.) and former Senator John Danforth (R-Mo.), tried in a small way, as did Congressman John Porter (R-Ill.), to start re-thinking Social Security. They wanted to privatize a small part of the system for the younger generations in order to build equity that can-not be taken from workers. Their solution was very simple. Just take 1.5 percent of the FICA tax withheld from each paycheck and invest it in IRAs for each individual. People's Social Security ben-efits would be adjusted for this program when they retire. In this way future retirees will not face the same frustration of relying on Social Security exclusively for retirement income. The commission was on the right track but the approach needed to be more drastic. A good start, but that is a political solution. The total answer lies in a new concept that gives current elders a continuing income as they have today, including cost-of-living-adjustments (COLAs) and at the same time provides a sound retirement for the working generations that follow.

Most politicians cling to the story that the trust funds will be de-pleted by 2029, or thereabouts. However, the real date to watch is 2002. This is the year where payments to recipients could very well start to exceed the actual revenues, according to several schedules in the 1995 Trustees Report. After this date Congress will be standing on the brink and will finally have to face the choice it has steadfastly refused to make, the decision that everyone knows is coming. The choices are very simple: raise FICA taxes or cut benefits. There are no other choices in the current scenario, *but there are other options.*

☆   ☆   ☆

It's rough enough these days to have the 6.2 percent taken out of your pay. Remember, the total deduction is 7.65 percent, of which 1.45 per-cent goes to Medicare. The worker's employer pays the other 7.65 percent. Those who are self-employed are hit with the entire 15.3 per-cent and are beginning to wonder just how fair that is.

Here's a real life situation to consider:

A group of young, successful romance novel writers gathered around the refreshment table during the break at their local writers group. Between them they had over forty published romance novels to their collective credit and were fast becoming well-known names in the field.

"You know, Barbara," Karen Leabo said, "This self-employment tax is killing me. That 15.3 percent I pay just eats up my royalties. However, I've started my own IRA since I doubt that I'll ever get much from Social Security when I retire in thirty years."

Karen Morrell chimed in: "You are so right. When my husband and I file our joint return, between the higher tax bracket and this 15 percent self-employment tax I have less than half of my royalties left. Heck of a way to do business."

"No kidding," Judy Christenberry added. "By the time *we* get to retirement, I doubt that there will be anything left in Social Security."

Liz Klingler put down her coffee and said, "I agree with you, Judy. After all that money we've been pumping into the system, you'd think they'd have money overflowing in the streets up there in Washington."

Barbara Harrison sighed, tossed her cup into the trash can and added, "We were sold a bill of goods by those politicians. It's too bad they don't know how to play it straight with us. A new retirement system is really needed for the generations to come."

"If they don't change things, we'll end up having to pay them to write," Judy muttered. They all nodded their collective heads. Maybe some day we'll get a break.

America is waiting.

To compound this problem the Republicans are now in control of both houses of Congress for the first time in forty years. They are doing their best to fulfill their promises when elected. They of course are so new to the reins of power and running things that the last thing they want to do is upset the elderly and their powerful allies such as the AARP.* Because of this attitude the country will lose two years of this golden opportunity to do something constructive for retirement programs.

We are not alone in this dilemma: Europe and Canada are right up there with us in thinking they can foolishly promise people everything in health care and retirement without planning how to finance the programs. It was recently reported that Belgium will have to raise its social security taxes 30 percent or cut benefits by the same amount within fifteen years if their program is to stay afloat. Italy and Germany are having similar problems and are learning that the government of a country cannot do everything for everyone.

Many learned economists such as Michael Tanner, project director for the Cato Institute in Washington, D.C.; Dr. Carolyn L. Weaver, Chief Economist, American Enterprise Institute in Washington, D.C.; Gary Becker, nobel laureate and Professor of Economics at the University of Chicago; and Robert Genetski, a noted economist from Chicago are now beginning to recommend that America look at the idea of privatizing its retirement systems, as a number of other countries have done in the past two decades. Chile has a system that is being looked at more and more these days, because it is doing a much better job than most other countries. They simply put younger workers on a system that took the withholding

---

*In 1958 the "self-proclaimed protector" of all American elders, the American Association of Retired Persons (AARP), was born. Through a collaboration between Ethel Percy Andrus, the seventy-two year old head of the National Retired Teachers Association (NRTA), and a young insurance executive named Leonard Davis, AARP was founded and its motive was steeped in the ethic of self-help. Its first mission was to enable the elderly to obtain private health insurance.

Today AARP, registered as nonprofit, has over $500 million in revenues and millions of members, all over age fifty. In 1995, AARP became the target of an investigation by Senator Alan Simpson (R-Wy.), chairman of the Senate subcommittee for Social Security. He was concerned that the AARP had overstepped its nonprofit status because much of its funds were coming from profit-making ventures.

and invested the money into income-producing vehicles. Those in retirement were taken care of by the government. They appropriated
the funds necessary each year for the elderly.

[Years ago privatization was looked upon as a crazy idea. It was
thought that no one could better take care of the elders than the government. But one idea came into being, as an oversight, that disturbed
those big-government idealists. Individual Retirement Accounts
(IRAs), initially designed to stimulate savings, proved to be a great
idea. Everyone loved them. When Congress first authorized that IRA
deposits could be deducted from a person's gross (pretax) income, this
savings concept grew so fast that Congress had to restrict it for fear of
losing a great deal of revenue.]

The overwhelming response to IRAs said two things. The people of this country know how to take care of themselves if given the
opportunity, and second, that Congress got scared that it might some-
day have to give up control of a very important way to garner votes.

When people such as University of Chicago economics professor and Nobel laureate Gary S. Becker espouse the privatization
idea and no one in government listens, you have to wonder. A good
example is how unions in Italy were all up in arms when the Italian
government wanted to make needed changes in their retirement system. Power and control are the key words in any language.

And then there is the Canadian situation. Their social programs
are broke. They ran up a debt of $550 billion by 1994, and this will
jump to $700 billion when the provinces are added. An example of
what is adding to this problem is that a Canadian can work just fourteen weeks a year and then spend the rest of the year drawing unemployment and other benefits. "We are in hock up to our eyeballs,"
Finance Minister Paul Martin told the House of Commons Finance
Committee in the fall of 1994. "That can't be sustained."

✯   ✯   ✯

A group of students at Stephen F. Austin State University in Nacog-doches, Texas, were asked to give their thoughts on Social Security. They graciously agreed and the following are their responses.

"I think Social Security is beneficial. I'm all for it. My brother receives it. He is special ed. David works at a restaurant sorting silverware. He gets over $300 a month from SSI* because my parents have to drive him around and he works less than twenty hours a week, though he has tried to work forty. My grandparents receive Social Security and I hope to receive it when I'm their age. They have put their money into Social Security and now they get it out, and they invested it so now they are well off."

Jill Coleman

"I think Social Security is a good thing. The elderly receive it now. I feel that they sometimes have not invested their money wisely, like mine and my parents' generation, and now have to fall back on Social Security in order to live in today's society, and I, myself, almost got it because of my head injury."

Dino Clark

"I don't know that much about Social Security. All I know is that they take it out of my paycheck every week, but I don't really know what they do with it."

Dana Bolden

"I don't like Social Security because the money I put into it I will never get back. They stick an IOU in my account and take my money

---

*This is Social Security Supplemental Income derived from Congressional appropriations.

to pay everyone Social Security when some people didn't put anything into the system."

Jennifer Harrison

"I think [social security] is good, because when I am older I want to get that money out to use because I won't work then."

Karen Crowder

"I think their heart was in the right place, but it hasn't worked out. I wish they would give me back the money that I put in so that I could invest for myself."

Kevin Hollis

These statements from young adults are a good cross section of the generation that is about to enter the work force and start the next step in their lives. At this point Social Security is not very often on their minds, and for that reason it is not well understood, nor even considered. To these young adults there is a whole new world ahead; retirement is still many years away. And as we know, most Americans of all ages have had these same dreams and thought these same thoughts.

The Jennifer Harrison story is a classic example of this emerging generation, and what could happen under a new set of circumstances, based on investment and compound interest growth. She is a bright, vivacious brunette of twenty, and a junior attending Stephen F. Austin University. Since she was sixteen Jennifer has been working part-time after school and in the summer to help pay for her college. In these four years she has paid over $2,000 in Social Security taxes. In today's Social Security world this money goes to the U.S. Treasury ostensibly to help pay for the retirement of today's elderly. A sound idea when the program first started, but within the coming decade the payment to elders will exceed the income from payroll taxes and then what will the spin-doctors in Washington come up with? What will the system say to Jennifer when she is ready to retire?

To solve Jennifer's retirement problem, as well as those of all working and retired Americans, let us delve into the world of compound interest and time. If this $2,000 withheld from Jennifer's salary had gone directly into a retirement account only for her, earning an average eight percent return and reinvesting all interest and dividends, at retirement time, forty-six years from now, Jennifer would have almost $80,000 in her fund account, from this $2,000 paid in her teen years. Can you visualize the total fund she would have at the end of her working days? Even if she took time out to get married and raise a family the money would still be hers; it would still be working for her and would be there when she retires.

Try that with today's Social Security system. It can't be done! Jennifer's money doesn't go to any account earmarked for her but instead is paid out to current recipients who paid into the system years ago.

Instead of presenting to the American people a Social Security system in a new form but with few substantive changes—in other words, rehashing the same tired old concept—we need to set our sights in a new direction. As time moves on, all things do change, and so will Social Security whether the system wants to or not. Recognizing this simple fact is sometimes very hard for those who have worked with the system for so long. But acknowledging this is what has made and keeps this country great and strong.

First it was the immigrants from Europe who had lofty dreams and suffered hardships and privations to come to this land in the hope of carving out a new country on the Atlantic shores. Next came the hardy pioneers who pushed west to open up the vast lands. As the country grew the Industrial Revolution came upon the scene, and its cause and effect were led by such giants of the day as Andrew Carnegie and John D. Rockefeller.

Andrew Carnegie was of Scottish descent and emigrated to this country in the mid 1800s. He first found work in a cotton factory, but looked forward to greater things. He amassed his fortune in oil and steel. His company, Carnegie Steel, merged into U.S. Steel to make it a giant in his day. He later became an important philanthropist, giving huge sums to countless schools, universities, and libraries. This was redistributing wealth for the benefit of all the citizens of this country without penalty.

John D. Rockefeller was from the same mold. He made his millions in oil and shared his wealth through foundations he set up. It took people like Carnegie and Rockefeller, not the government, to lead this country to greatness. People-driven investments amass wealth, governments do not. The current government-run Social Security is based on taxes, now regressive in nature, and can never succeed in its goal. Redistribution of wealth is an idea as old as the Pyramids and has never succeeded.

During the 1992 presidential campaign Ross Perot said, "If you want your government to come *from the people* and *not at the people,* then let your vote say so." That is what the people of this country must realize if the problems of retirement, which include Social Security, are to be brought to a sound financial conclusion, without penalty to anyone.

Fortunately, the newspaper and magazine stories are beginning to educate people of all generations and to stir things up. The kettle is beginning to boil up and overheat. The full realization of the seriousness of these problems may soon spill over with very significant consequences.

As unofficial spokespersons for this emerging adult generation, Jennifer and Kevin clearly and succinctly indict the overloaded Social Security system and those who manage it. Will Congress ever stand up and show this new generation that, as its representatives, too, they want the best for America's children and grandchildren?

Using examples from history as guides can at times save us a great deal of grief when there are very serious problems confronting us. For instance, during America's Industrial Revolution there came a man who championed the cause of the common worker. Samuel Gompers was one of the original and dynamic labor leaders of the early days of unionism. Gompers was a genius at handling people and at building and organizing unions. He helped to organize a number of unions and was one of the founders of the American Federation of Labor (AFL) in 1886, serving as its president for many years thereafter.

He firmly believed and fought hard for better working conditions and wages for the common worker, and abhorred socialism in any form. Socialism—the view that it is the responsibility of government to redistribute wealth to benefit the less well off— was a force in both unions and politics at the turn of the twentieth century. Gompers rejected any idea of combining socialism with an attempt to integrate labor into the mainstream of American capitalism. Gomperism, though, was the beginning of pressure group trade unionism, a path that led inevitably to today's interest group politics.

Even so, Gompers effectively integrated labor into American capitalist society. His goal was respectability for labor through agreement between the laborer and capitalism. He also believed that American labor would achieve it outside the corrupting influence of politics. He concluded, if labor was to contribute to a bettering of society, it would be under its own steam.

Gompers and President Roosevelt had many things in common: both were Democrats who believed in the common people, and both men believed in offering a helping hand, but basically they felt that people should be given the opportunity to stand on their own two feet. To their way of thinking big government was never meant to do any more than just that, offer a helping hand.

Perhaps Congress would do well to remember what Samuel Gompers said in 1915:

> Doing for people what they can and ought to do for themselves is a dangerous experiment. In the last analysis the welfare of the workers depends upon their own initiative. Whatever is done under the guise of philanthropy or social morality which in any way lessens initiative is the greatest crime that can be committed against toilers. Let social busy-bodies and professional "public morals experts" in their fads reflect upon the perils they rashly invite under this pretense of social welfare.

5

Baby Boomers on the Way to Bust

"Whenever the people are well informed they can be trusted with their own government; that whenever things get so far wrong as to attract their notice, they may be relied on to set them to rights."

Thomas Jefferson, 1789

Three years ago, in 1992, the voters, following this tenet of Thomas Jefferson, told Congress in no uncertain terms that they wanted change. They elected a Democrat president for the first time in twelve years and sent 110 new men and women to Congress. All these new lawmakers went to Washington, but promptly forgot why the voters had sent them. They just continued on with the same "business as usual" that had been going on for nearly forty years. Seeing that nothing was going to change with the Democratic leadership in charge, the voters on November 8, 1994, sent them packing and installed a Republican Congress for the first time in four decades. The quietly growing Social Security deficits from the fifties through the seventies culminated in 1980 when the system went bankrupt. This crisis was resolved by raising the Social Security tax rates to such a point that they developed surpluses for future years. Instead of setting these surplus funds aside, Congress used them and left the system worse than before; not only was Social Security facing huge expenditures for those claiming benefits, it now had an enormous debt as well. And to compound the problem our representatives exercised little, if any, foresight or planning with the Social Security system. They just crossed their fingers and hoped no one would ask them about the future of this fine system that was slowly but surely sinking under its own weight as more retirees were living longer and the cost-of-living-adjustments were adding an unrealized burden.

One of the results of World War II was what we now call the Baby Boomer generation. Millions of children were born in the decade after the war, and for a period of time in the seventies and eighties this was a financial shot in the arm for Social Security. The Baby Boomers were entering the work place and all those new Social Security taxes were now flowing into the system. At the same time, the aging population whose members were retiring and making claims on the Social Security system were down in numbers. They had lived through the struggle of the Great Depression and had seen their numbers dwindle as a result of war casualties. Also medicine was not as sophisticated during the early decades of this century, and many died of illnesses long since eradicated.

What could be better, Social Security was well taken care of and with the huge jump in the Social Security tax rates of the early eighties, a big surplus was there for Congress to use as it desired. What could be better?

But time doesn't stand still. The eventual aging of the Baby Boomers was moving forward slowly like a glacier. Nothing could stop it and yet Congress was interested in the here and now rather than the future. That worry was for tomorrow. Well tomorrow is nearly here, and right at the very beginning of a new century, in the year 2002, the monies paid out to Social Security recipients will exceed the actual revenues. Oh there will be paper interest on the government securities that the trust funds purchase and all sorts of accounting adjustments, but that will be the approximate year when things will really begin to change.

How much of a potential burden will the Baby Boomers be to the Social Security system in the early years of the next century? Let's see.

World War II was the precipitating catalyst that turned the United States into a global power without peer. One ancillary effect of this phenomenon was the beginning of the age of technology. Television, communications and the jet age were just some of the exciting advances that led the way into this new era. We turned our eyes to space: America's astronauts set foot on the moon, while others made satellites circle the earth. Knowledge became the driving force as never before.

During this era the Baby Boomers were born. This huge influx of children, eighty million strong, born during the roughly ten years following the war, remained unnoticed through the next four decades as these youngsters grew to maturity. Our lawmakers ignored the signs along the way but eventually realized that there was a huge human surge rumbling throughout the land from New England to California, a potential social tidal wave that within the next several decades could swamp the entire retirement program.

At the same time Congress turned on the money tap. In the 1960s and 1970s Social Security began to flow in greater increases than ever before, but little planning was ever done to increase tax revenues to compensate. It wasn't until the early eighties that our lawmakers admitted that Social Security had reached the crisis stage.

The system was "fixed" by raising Social Security taxes, increasing the tax base by including federal employees, and closing loop holes that allowed other governmental entities, such as cities

and counties, to opt out of Social Security in favor of their own retirement systems.

Congress went one step further: it included a provision in its
1983 bill that the retirement age would rise from sixty-five to sixty-
seven over a period of time. Many feel that this should be increased
to age seventy since it is currently estimated that the average life expectancy is now seventy-five years, according to long-range actuar-
ial estimates developed for the 1995 Social Security Trustees Report,
and this will continue to increase over the next several decades.
Economists also like to point out that when sixty-five was selected
as the optional retirement age the life expectancy was only sixty one
years. Increasing the age of retirement solves the problem of financing the system by telling the younger generations that they will
be taken care of but only when they are almost at death's door. Retirement should be a time to sit back and enjoy the fruits of life's
labors. If elders want to do something new or travel to see the wonders of this country and the many lands beyond, they should be able
to do so without the government trying to make it harder for them to
reach these goals.

Is it any wonder, then, that a new system is needed. A system that
will let the elderly enjoy their retirement years. At age sixty-five
there are for the most of us a number of years ahead, and they should
be good years, not ones filled with never-ending financial concerns
about survival.

To add a twist to the story, Congress raised the Social Security
withholding (FICA) tax rates high enough to bring about large surpluses for the better part of three decades. The idea was great because Congress also realized that borrowing these surpluses would
hide the true government deficit each year and the national debt. To
illustrate: in 1995 the administration says there will be a $165 billion
deficit, but in this same fiscal year approximately $50 billion (all the
surplus) was borrowed from the four Social Security Trust Funds.
This $50 billion IOU, when added to the $165 billion deficit gives a

real deficit of $215 billion for the fiscal year. That's the dirty little secret that no one in Washington wants to talk about, and of course there would never have to be a payback. When the Social Security system needs more money Congress will either increase the FICA tax or reduce benefits or both.

Explanations will flow and Congress will send out its best speakers to tell everyone that things are just great. Later on they could just tell the workers it was necessary to raise the Social Security tax rates again, but the average Americans are catching on.

With Social Security funding problems looming on the horizon, Congressman Andy Jacobs (D-Ind.), Chairman of the Subcommittee on Social Security, held a hearing on September 21, 1993, titled "Can Baby Boomers Afford to Retire?" Little did Congressman Jacobs realize that one year later all the key Congressional players would change. New politicians would take up the challenge that the Democrats had refused to consider for so long.

This hearing in 1993 was in reality a hearing not only on the Baby Boomers, but also on the future of the Social Security system in its present form. Why the hearings and concern at this time? Because there were some 80 million working people in this boomer generation and it will cause a tremendous strain on the Social Security system when they start to retire in two decades.*

The Congressional Budget Office (CBO) cited the Social Security Trustees Report of 1993 and concluded that the Old Age Survivors Insurance Trust Fund would not likely be exhausted until the year 2044. The CBO further said early signs suggested that Baby Boomers would enjoy higher incomes in retirement than their parents, but this does not mean retirement will meet the expectations of this aging population.

Director Reischauer's testimony was of great interest to all at-

---

*Of course it's not too difficult to comprehend that these aging Americans comprised a huge voting bloc that could be very unhappy if something wasn't done to correct the system before they reach retirement age.

tending this hearing. It was thought by all that the director would include all phases of the problem. Paul Hewitt, Vice President of National Taxpayers Union Foundation, was later to say in his testimony before the committee: "We find it curious, therefore, that in shaping the scope of the study the committee precluded CBO from looking at the effects of entitlements on the budget."

Congressman Jim Bunning (R-Ky.), then ranking minority member, understood what was going on and questioned the validity of the CBO report. Mr. Bunning further said that the long-term insolvency of the trust funds (that's quite an admission) would cause problems within the lifetime of many in this generation. He added, "I do not think that saying something may have to be done is very accurate. Something must be done; the question is what and when." During this hearing Mr. Bunning asked Reischauer about his assumption that adjustments to benefits may be necessary. Reischauer just took a deep breath, rolled his eyes and said, "Long-term projections were difficult." Reischauer concluded his remarks by saying, "But just how much better off than current retirees Baby Boomers will be when they reach retirement is still an open question."

The real story of that landmark 1993 congressional hearing is that the Congress still did not realize that the path it had been taking with Social Security was coming to an end. The Old Guard on Capitol Hill was convinced that if it kept the elderly content with their retirement benefits the incumbent senators and congresspersons would continue receiving the vote of this powerful group. With an increasing number of middle-aged workers questioning the likelihood that Social Security would be there when they reached retirement, all the concern about Social Security became more widespread and pronounced. No voter or worker in this country believes Social Security can continue on the same course it is on today. From Boston to San Francisco, the younger generation simply does not believe the explanations that come out of Washington these days. The simple truth is the numbers just don't add up any longer. That anyone in Congress or the administration could look the people in the eye and tell them that Social Security is in great shape is unthinkable, yet there are still those in Washington who believe their own rhetoric.

Just a few short years ago a company was formed in the Midwest to sell slenderizing products. This product did a good job. Their sales organization was structured in a many tiered system to give those who get in the game first great rewards. Approximately two-thirds of the selling price was split among many sales people and managers in a down line chain. This classic scheme worked well for several years. The top sales managers kept telling everyone how wonderful the product was (and it was a good product) and how great the future looked. But like an inverted pyramid, everyone concentrated on the sales apparatus rather than the product. The organization became too heavy for the small customer base and eventually collapsed on itself. Outside pressures also hastened its downfall because other companies sold the product at one-third the price.

There is simply no way such a scheme can work over the long haul. That is what Social Security is fast becoming, and it can no longer be stopped. The 1994 Trustees Report runs the estimated benefits figures out to trillions of dollars in several decades. By then, with the government owing trillions to the Trust Funds, just how stable will the Social Security system be and what will we be able to expect? It isn't realistic to expect the economy to continually expand and generate enough new jobs to support the growing population of elders. Germany, Brazil and Mexico have proven that when systems get way out of kilter and rampant inflation rears its ugly head, then someone will pay a very heavy price. The American worker now knows this, but feels powerless to stop the growing financial tide that could very easily swamp the entire system.

Where do Mr. Reischauer and his staff come up with all the figures to make this report work? There is no doubt that future generations should do well. But there will always be the less fortunate in any society. That is the nature of humankind. There is no changing this, because in many cases no amount of pushing or cajoling will put the ambition or desire into some people. We will always have those who want to live off the dole, and the federal government has turned into a patsy for that type of game.

The enormity of the national debt and the constantly rising budget deficit are close to overwhelming the thinking and reasoning of Congress and the administration. They want people to save for their retirement and yet they are looking for anything and everything to tax, as the need seems limitless. To back away from this precipitous path is perhaps the best thing to do. Investment and growth do not come from Washington, with its self-defeating regressive taxing policies. It is time for those inside the beltway to listen to the American people.

The 1993 Congressional hearing on the Baby Boomers' retirement included a number of leading experts: James Klein with the Association of Private Pension Plans, Martha Priddy with KPMG Peat Marwick; Cindy Hounsell with the Pension Rights Center; and Paul Hewitt leading Social Security and tax expert with the National Taxpayers Union Foundation. These experts shook their heads at the CBO report.

James Klein remarked, "My message is simple. Unless Congress and the executive branch immediately cease enacting policies like the reduction of compensation limits for plan contributions and benefits and grant relief from onerous regulatory burdens, then congressional hearings and other efforts to draw attention to the retirement needs of the Baby Boomers will just be a hollow gesture. Congress cannot simply voice its support for a strong retirement system and then proceed to enact measures which undermine that very goal."

Can there be any message that is easier to understand, and yet

Congress doesn't even seem to notice what is going on in the world around it. Many of the younger Baby Boomers liked the idea of Individual Retirement Accounts (IRAs) in which tax-deferred contributions could be made up to $2,000 for an individual and $4,000 for a couple. But because this incentive to save and invest reduced tax revenues, Congress just couldn't have it, so the IRA legislation was modified to reduce its tax advantage. Not surprisingly, fewer people entered IRAs or continued to contribute to them. Government is not hard to understand. When all these bureaucrats are hired who then have vested interests in what goes on, rules and regulations sprout up like weeds in your front lawn. Add to this the fact that both houses of Congress are given pension plans that are five times as good as Social Security and each elected official has one more reason to remain in office. Somewhere along the line the people who this whole government was set up to help seem to have been forgotten.

But let's continue with the subcommittee hearings that were held to show concern, but were never planned to go anywhere.

Martha Priddy of KPMG Peat Marwick came right to the point: "If you want to continue to encourage employer provided plans, you need to stop changing the law." She ended by saying this forces employers to terminate plans and when they do more pressure is placed in the Social Security system.

Cindy Hounsell of the Pension Rights Center then pointed out, "The CBO study masks the reality that in fact all is not well with today's retirees and that unless current policies are reversed, their children will fare even worse when they reach retirement age. She concluded that, "the problem is that these workers, moderate- and low-income individuals unable to save voluntarily for themselves, are the very people our heavily taxed, subsidized private retirement system is meant to serve."

Paul Hewitt of the National Taxpayers Union Foundation summed it up well: "Our blunt assessment, on reviewing this report, is that it is fig leaf time again on Capitol Hill. That the Ways and

Means Committee is examining the Baby Boomers' future is heartening, but that CBO wore blinders and produced an unjustifiably optimistic assessment is dismaying. Every American knows that the baby boom is a very large cohort and when its members retire, it will place an enormous strain on our system's old age benefits." Hewitt went on to say,

> The CBO knows that Congress will have to enact a tax increase equal in size to the one it passed earlier this summer (1993) every four years for the next half century just to keep pace with the projected growth in the entitlements. In our survey, only 4 percent of respondents strongly agreed that government can be trusted to manage Social Security and Medicare.
>
> The poll found that entitlements are no longer the sacred cow politicians believe them to be. Some 62 percent of respondents preferred cutting benefits to new tax increases. The facts simply do not support an optimistic assessment. By basing its conclusions on incomplete information, the CBO's report only erodes further the public's already tenuous faith in government.

Congressman John Porter (D-Ill.), realizing what the future holds related his thinking. "Social Security is at a crossroads. Returning to pay-as-you-go financing sets up tomorrow's workers for huge tax increases. If left unchecked, current law governing the Trust Fund reserve will cause a serious fiscal crisis when the Baby Boomers retire."

Then Committee Chairman Jacobs ended the 1993 hearing with these words:

> So, help us solve human nature. Help us solve the bleak fact that many people, as one witness said, do live from paycheck to paycheck and don't have two copper pennies to save in a year's time; maybe they even borrow against next year's wages for current expenses.
>
> In the end, democracies have a terrible problem because they re-

quire self-discipline on the part of each autonomous individual, each owner of the corporation, each participant. . . .

In June 1989 Karen Meredith, a certified public accountant, saw the many problems looming on the horizon for the Social Security system, especially when the working men and women of her baby boom generation begin to retire. To address these concerns, she formed an organization now known as the American Association of Boomers (AAB) in Irving, Texas. The group has grown to over twenty-five thousand members but in 1994 its growth slowed a bit. The Baby Boomers remain basically unorganized. At present they are in their prime and are not worrying about retirement. Once they start reaching age fifty (in about ten years) they will begin to think about this problem in a serious way. They will then look to the organization of older persons like the American Association of Retired Persons (AARP). If they had read the AAB brochure they might have second thoughts. Part of this brochure says:

> Experts are predicting that the aging of the Boomer generation will precipitate a monumental financial crisis sometime between 2010 and 2020 that will imperil the economic well-being of our nation for generations to come.
>
> Federal trust funds are nothing more than accounting gimmicks. Today's workers are paying huge Social Security taxes for nothing but a financial "disaster-in-the-making."

They sum up by saying, "The AAB mission is for lasting changes, leaving a positive legacy for generations to come."

This thinking runs directly counter to the AARP's view that the Social Security Trust Funds are sound and there will be no problems for at least fifty years on the current course, as cited in recent newspaper articles and magazines.

Another factor has to be considered when discussing the financial problem that the Baby Boomers face with the Social Security system. Recent studies at a number of prominent universities suggest that Social Security experts are grossly underestimating how long the people of this generation are likely to live. Earlier we mentioned that retirement was initially set at sixty-five because few people lived, on average, much beyond the age of sixty-one. Later, as medical care and longevity improved, the average length of a human life increased to seventy-five, fully ten years longer than initially anticipated. Baby boomers will live far longer because they are heeding many medical studies on the causes of diseases: their lower fat and cholesterol intake will improve their lives and increase their longevity even more. This generation understands better than any other that in addition to watching one's food intake, a sound fitness program is also essential.

Now we are finding out that these health programs have another side to them, and strangely enough it's a negative from the perspective of Social Security. In today's world, if you plan to live a long and happy life you'd better plan on developing an individual retirement program beyond any likely government benefits, because the current Social Security system will not be able to handle the increased financial burden after the next several decades. As we've pointed out, after 2002 the tide begins to turn as Social Security starts paying out more in actual dollars than it takes in. To raise payroll taxes to the point needed to pay the boomer retirees is out of the question. Would anyone stand still for doubling their FICA taxes? The only other choice is to cut benefits, but such a suggestion would have AARP descending on Washington like a plague.

As Assistant Secretary of Aging for Health and Human Services Torres-Gil said, "We have a short window of opportunity to avert such a crisis." Such opportunities just don't come along everyday. When they do—and one window is here now for the next several years—Congress had better take advantage of the opportunity or it may not get another chance without paying a much higher price. The sad part of this is that the American people, especially the elderly, will be the real losers, paying an even higher price. This choice has been given to the Republicans now that they control both houses of Congress. America's voters have demonstrated that they are fed up with inaction; they want a solution that will end the constant frustration they have felt all these years.

How many of us have sat around wringing our hands and kicking ourselves for not taking advantage of an opportunity. This problem is not yet on the Republican agenda—and it may never be—but there is a sound answer.

6

The Amazing, Vanishing
Trust Fund Surplus

"I am for a government rigorously frugal & simple, applying all possible savings of the public revenue to the discharge of the national debt; and not for a multiplication of officers & salaries merely to make partisans, & for increasing, by every device, the public debt, on the principle of it's being a public blessing."

Thomas Jefferson, 1799

Could anyone have said it better today? The Shakespearean tragedy that is going on in Washington these days makes the average person wonder if our politicians and bureaucrats really believe the rhetoric they are putting out in defense of their indefensible position on Social Security.

We've all seen the famous magician and illusionist David Copperfield make trains disappear, fly like a bird, or just simply cut a pretty girl in half, then later on put her back together again, with no effort at all.

The people who tell you there is a Social Security Trust Fund surplus of any kind must have been trained in a similar school. True, there are IOUs from the U.S. Treasury, or if you prefer, bonds that can never be sold to anyone, and of course they draw mythical interest that will never be paid. These bonds and the interest can only be redeemed by the U.S. Treasury. ("Redeemed" is not really the appropriate word, because from the beginning the interest had never been there in a physical form.) Assuming any redemption of bonds actually takes place, it could only be accomplished after receiving approval and funding from Congress. And where will Congress get the money? You guessed it. From you and me! The government could borrow the money by selling more Treasury bonds, but such a large drain on available money in the economy would probably push the country into a recession. When the government borrows money in the open market it leaves less available for companies and individuals to borrow for private needs. The government could just print more money to buy back the Social Security Treasury bonds, but that could lead to inflation. It's only other option is to raise additional taxes. So, in seven years get ready to see your paycheck to take a huge dip. Your money is going south if you still want to hang on to a pipe dream that once was a sound retirement system.

Social Security retirees are just holding their collective breaths, hoping they still will get their monthly payments that average $700. And all those ex-congressmen aren't giving a second thought to getting a Social Security check because they have their own retirement plan (see chapter 11).

The trustees of the Social Security system would also like us to believe that all is well. They put out a report each year telling (estimating and hoping may be better words) how sound the system is. They provide countless facts and figures, enough to confuse everyone except the most dedicated economist. Let me give you an example of how they tell the story. Below is their most current Trustee Report dated April 12, 1994, which the future Social Security Trust Fund surplus balances.

1996—$555.1 billion
1997— 624.2 billion
1998— 697.8 billion
1999— 776.4 billion
2000—$861.1 billion

The trustees claim that by the year 2020 the surplus will reach a high of $2,975.9 trillion. With that kind of money in the system what could we possibly have to worry about? We should all sit back, kick off our shoes and relax. We're being well taken care of.

Just one question, though, before we do. In the 1993 Trustees Report, the year 2020 reads out at $4,674.9 trillion. What happened? In just one year the Trustees have had to revise the surplus for 2020 downward by $1,699 trillion. Who is doing the estimating and how far off are they?

But the trustees also forgot to tell the American people—in fact, they never do tell us—that these huge surpluses are in mythical, nonnegotiable bonds, and the only way they can ever be used is for Congress to increase taxes—either income or Social Security taxes, it doesn't matter which, because it's all paid by the working people of this country.

How would you like to have 12.4 percent FICA tax taken out of your pay rather than the 6.2 percent that currently comes out? That's a 100 percent increase in the tax. That would amount to about $60 a week for a person making $25,000 per year. That amounts to $3,120 per year.

In effect, all working men and women will be paying for their Social Security retirement benefits twice after the year 2002. Years ago Social Security worked well because Congress had not tapped into the surplus. In 1983 they began the long road to bankruptcy for the second time in a generation. By forcing the Social Security Trust Fund to buy Treasury bonds, the government has assured that a financial crisis awaits when repayment of the bonds comes due. As the years have gone by more and more people now realize what has been going on. It becomes harder each year for the politicians to justify what they are doing, just to keep the annual deficit down.

The Democratic administration has been bragging that in fiscal 1994 the deficit was only $193 billion. But that wasn't the case because they used $58 billion from the Social Security Trust Funds to arrive at this figure. The actual deficit was $251 billion.

The Republicans in the March 1995 debate should have taken those two North Dakota senators at their word and promised no more fooling around with Social Security and gotten them to vote for the balanced budget amendment. The simple fact is neither the Democrats nor the Republicans will be able to fiddle around with these Trust Fund surpluses after the year 2002, because there won't be anything to fool around with. What gets paid out will exceed what is expected to come in. Then a whole new set of problems will come into being, and the spin doctors in our nation's capitol will once again set to work to allay the fears of the masses.

Perhaps the newly elected Republican Congress will learn this tragic lesson from the Democrats and put a stop to this thinking. The Entitlements Commission that was recently chaired by Senator Bob Kerrey (D-Neb.) and former Senator John Danforth, that has gone the way of many other commissions, was in reality the first step out of this wasteland of debt and increased taxes toward a sound retirement program that doesn't exhaust the resources of the federal government.

Over the past decade many prominent people, writers, and columnists have written and spoken on this growing problem. During the summer and fall of 1992 the number of stories published increased. Many outlined the different problems Congress has brought on itself by borrowing the Social Security surpluses.

As an example, in fiscal 1992 the U.S. Treasury borrowed over $50 billion from the Social Security Trust Funds (the entire surplus) and in return gave them these now famous non-negotiable bonds to cover the amount. Stop and think. Did you ever give yourself an IOU, and then later pay it back? Sounds crazy doesn't it. That's what Congress wants you to believe it is doing. Is it any wonder that average Americans throughout the country are very skeptical?

The Social Security Trust Funds are now the proud possessor of over $400 billion worth of these unique government bonds (IOUs), and by the year 2000 the funds should have close to $1 trillion worth. At that time the interest the government should be paying will be running over $80 billion annually. For those readers who find this just a bit hard to fathom, I have reproduced just one statement of account for the Federal Old Age & Survivor's Insurance Trust Fund of the Social Security Administration dated June 30, 1995.

DESCRIPTION OF HOLDINGS AS OF 06/30/95
INVESTED BALANCE: $446,142,674,000.00

MATURITY DATE	U.S. TREASURY SECURITIES	AMOUNT
June 30, 1999	13¾% Bonds	$1,491,915,000.00
June 30, 1998	13¾% Bonds	469,685,000.00
June 30, 1997	13¾% Bonds	469,685,000.00
June 30, 1996	13¾% Bonds	469,684,000.00
June 30, 1998	10¾% Bonds	1,022,230,000-00
June 30, 1997	10¾% Bonds	1,022,230,000.00
June 30, 1996	10¾% Bonds	1,022,231,000.00
June 30, 2000	10⅜% Bonds	2,057,101,000.00
June 30, 1999	10⅜% Bonds	565,186,000-00
June 30, 1998	10⅜% Bonds	565,186,000-00
June 30, 1997	10⅜% Bonds	565,186,000.00
June 30, 1996	10⅜% Bonds	565,186,000.00
June 30, 2003	9¼% Bonds	5,912,435,000.00
June 30, 2002	9¼% Bonds	2,240,308,000.00
June 30, 2001	9¼% Bonds	2,240,308,000.00
June 30, 2000	9¼% Bonds	$2,240,309,000.00

MATURITY DATE	U.S. TREASURY SECURITIES	AMOUNT
June 30, 1999	$9\frac{1}{4}$% Bonds	$ 2,240,309,000.00
June 30, 1998	$9\frac{1}{4}$% Bonds	2,240,309,000.00
June 30, 1997	$9\frac{1}{4}$% Bonds	2,240,309,000.00
June 30, 1996	$9\frac{1}{4}$% Bonds	2,240,309,000.00
June 30, 2005	$8\frac{3}{4}$% Bonds	13,012,238,000.00
June 30, 2004	$8\frac{3}{4}$% Bonds	13,012,238,000.00
June 30, 2003	$8\frac{3}{4}$% Bonds	7,099,803,000.00
June 30, 2002	$8\frac{3}{4}$% Bonds	7,099,803,000.00
June 30, 2001	$8\frac{3}{4}$% Bonds	7,099,803,000.00
June 30, 2000	$8\frac{3}{4}$% Bonds	7,099,802,000.00
June 30, 1999	$8\frac{3}{4}$% Bonds	7,099,802,000.00
June 30, 1998	$8\frac{3}{4}$% Bonds	7,099,802,000.00
June 30, 1997	$8\frac{3}{4}$% Bonds	7,099,802,000.00
June 30, 1996	$8\frac{3}{4}$% Bonds	7,099,802,000.00
June 30, 2002	$8\frac{5}{8}$% Bonds	3,672,127,000.00
June 30, 2001	$8\frac{5}{8}$% Bonds	1,301,731,000.00
June 30, 2000	$8\frac{5}{8}$% Bonds	1,301,731,000.00
June 30, 1999	$8\frac{5}{8}$% Bonds	1,301,731,000.00
June 30, 1998	$8\frac{5}{8}$% Bonds	1,301,731,000.00
June 30, 1997	$8\frac{5}{8}$% Bonds	1,301,731,000.00
June 30, 1996	$8\frac{5}{8}$% Bonds	1,301,731,000.00
June 30, 2001	$8\frac{3}{8}$% Bonds	2,370,396,000.00
June 30, 2000	$8\frac{3}{8}$% Bonds	313,295,000.00
June 30, 1999	$8\frac{3}{8}$% Bonds	313,295,000.00
June 30, 1998	$8\frac{3}{8}$% Bonds	313,295,000.00
June 30, 1997	$8\frac{3}{8}$% Bonds	313,295,000.00
June 30, 1996	$8\frac{3}{8}$% Bonds	313,295,000.00
June 30, 2006	$8\frac{1}{8}$% Bonds	16,623,586,000.00
June 30, 2005	$8\frac{1}{8}$% Bonds	3,611,348,000.00
June 30, 2004	$8\frac{1}{8}$% Bonds	3,611,348,000.00
June 30, 2003	$8\frac{1}{8}$% Bonds	$ 3,611,348,000.00

MATURITY DATE	U.S. TREASURY SECURITIES	AMOUNT
June 30, 2002	8⅛% Bonds	$ 3,611,348,000.00
June 30, 2001	8⅛% Bonds	3,611,348,000.00
June 30, 2000	8⅛% Bonds	3,611,349,000.00
June 30, 1999	8⅛% Bonds	3,611,349,000.00
June 30, 1998	8⅛% Bonds	3,611,349,000.00
June 30, 1997	8⅛% Bonds	3,611,349,000.00
June 30, 1996	8⅛% Bonds	3,611,349,000.00
June 30, 2007	7⅜% Bonds	20,199,060,000.00
June 30, 2006	7⅜% Bonds	3,575,474,000.00
June 30, 2005	7⅜% Bonds	3,575,474,000.00
June 30, 2004	7⅜% Bonds	3,575,474,000.00
June 30, 2003	7⅜% Bonds	3,575,474,000.00
June 30, 2002	7⅜% Bonds	3,575,474,000.00
June 30, 2001	7⅜% Bonds	3,575,474,000.00
June 30, 2000	7⅜% Bonds	3,575,473,000.00
June 30, 1999	7⅜% Bonds	3,575,473,000.00
June 30, 1998	7⅜% Bonds	3,575,473,000.00
June 30, 1997	7⅜% Bonds	3,575,473,000.00
June 30, 1996	7⅜% Bonds	3,575,473,000.00
June 30, 2009	7¼% Bonds	27,311,591,000.00
June 30, 2008	7¼% Bonds	3,961,557,000.00
June 30, 2007	7¼% Bonds	3,961,557,000.00
June 30, 2006	7¼% Bonds	3,961,556,000.00
June 30, 2005	7¼% Bonds	3,961,556,000.00
June 30, 2004	7¼% Bonds	3,961,556,000.00
June 30, 2003	7¼% Bonds	3,961,556,000.00
June 30, 2002	7¼% Bonds	3,961,556,000.00
June 30, 2001	7¼% Bonds	3,961,556,000.00
June 30, 2000	7¼% Bonds	3,961,556,000.00
June 30, 1999	7¼% Bonds	3,961,556,000.00
June 30, 1998	7¼% Bonds	$ 3,961,557,000.00

MATURITY DATE	U.S. TREASURY SECURITIES	AMOUNT
June 30, 1997	$7\frac{1}{4}\%$ Bonds	$ 3,961,557,000.00
June 30, 1996	$7\frac{1}{4}\%$ Bonds	3,961,557,000.00
June 30, 2010	$6\frac{1}{2}\%$ Bonds	29,742,844,000.00
June 30, 2009	$6\frac{1}{2}\%$ Bonds	2,431,254,000.00
June 30, 2008	$6\frac{1}{2}\%$ Bonds	2,431,254,000.00
June 30, 2007	$6\frac{1}{2}\%$ Bonds	2,431,254,000.00
June 30, 2006	$6\frac{1}{2}\%$ Bonds	2,431,254,000.00
June 30, 2005	$6\frac{1}{2}\%$ Bonds	2,431,254,000.00
June 30, 2004	$6\frac{1}{2}\%$ Bonds	2,431,254,000.00
June 30, 2003	$6\frac{1}{2}\%$ Bonds	2,431,254,000.00
June 30, 2002	$6\frac{1}{2}\%$ Bonds	2,431,254,000.00
June 30, 2001	$6\frac{1}{2}\%$ Bonds	2,431,254,000.00
June 30, 2000	$6\frac{1}{2}\%$ Bonds	2,431,254,000.00
June 30, 1999	$6\frac{1}{2}\%$ Bonds	2,431,254,000.00
June 30, 1998	$6\frac{1}{2}\%$ Bonds	2,431,253,000.00
June 30, 1997	$6\frac{1}{2}\%$ Bonds	2,431,253,000.00
June 30, 1996	$6\frac{1}{2}\%$ Bonds	2,671,770,000.00
June 30, 2008	$6\frac{1}{4}\%$ Bonds	23,350,034,000.00
June 30, 2007	$6\frac{1}{4}\%$ Bonds	3,150,974,000.00
June 30, 2006	$6\frac{1}{4}\%$ Bonds	3,150,975,000.00
June 30, 2005	$6\frac{1}{4}\%$ Bonds	3,150,975,000.00
June 30, 2004	$6\frac{1}{4}\%$ Bonds	3,150,975,000.00
June 30, 2003	$6\frac{1}{4}\%$ Bonds	3,150,975,000.00
June 30, 2002	$6\frac{1}{4}\%$ Bonds	3,150,975,000.00
June 30, 2001	$6\frac{1}{4}\%$ Bonds	3,150,975,000.00
June 30, 2000	$6\frac{1}{4}\%$ Bonds	3,150,975,000.00
June 30, 1999	$6\frac{1}{4}\%$ Bonds	3,150,975,000.00
June 30 1998	$6\frac{1}{4}\%$ Bonds	3,150,975,000.00
June 30, 1997	$6\frac{1}{4}\%$ Bonds	3,150,975,000.00
June 30, 1996	$6\frac{1}{4}\%$ Bonds	$ 2,910,458,000.00

Let's follow the paper trail of these trust funds.

The simple fact of the matter is that there really isn't and never have been any Social Security Trust Funds, except possibly on paper. All the money the government takes in, in any form, be it income taxes, FICA taxes, fees, and the like goes directly to the U.S. Treasury where it is used to pay the general bills of the government. This includes all monthly Social Security payments to recipients, as well as all welfare payments. The bureaucratic talk about Social Security being "off budget" (set aside from the government's general revenue and earmarked for Social Security payouts) or "on budget" (actually included in annual government budgets as a form of revenue and expenditure) has no substance.

This fairy tale surplus started in 1983 as a result of Congress fixing a Social Security system that had gone broke. After a great deal of posturing lawmakers raised the FICA rates to the point where they would technically have a surplus in the Social Security Trust Funds for about twenty-six years. It was projected that for this time period more money would be coming into the funds than would be paid out. During this period they knew they could do just what they pleased with the surpluses, because the monies weren't separated from general revenue and because the day of reckoning seemed so many years away. They could worry about paying the money back later. Well, the day of reckoning has almost arrived.

Thomas Jefferson was so right when he said, "public debt is the greatest of the dangers to be feared from government." If the government had played it straight with the monies paid into Social Security and really made them trust funds, it could have taken the surplus funds and invested them in income-producing vehicles. The interest alone would now be in the billions. Some legislators feared that if such a plan were put in place, then the government would be in a position to own part of the private sector and this would pose a serious conflict of interest. But that concern was just smoke screen. These fears could have been allayed by putting the funds in the hands of independent money managers.

Had such an investment option been exercised, the dividends on the $400 billion plus the Trust Funds would now exceed $32 billion each year. With this type of real funding there would have been no need in recent years to increase FICA taxes in order to maintain the present retirement levels for all current recipients. In fact, Congress might have been able to *reduce* the tax rates. That's called planning for the future, which is what Congress should be all about, at least when it comes to Social Security.

There are still many columnists and newsletter writers who promote the idea that there will be no collapse of the Social Security system, and quite frankly they are right. However, the price to keep it afloat at current benefit levels will be a steep one, unless we choose to adjust benefits or the rates of increase for COLAs. In either case it will not be a pleasant choice for lawmakers.

Many still say that the Trust Funds are solvent and the surplus is still growing. They say this surplus is invested in Treasury bonds, which are as safe an investment as you can buy today. But as we have already seen, these bonds are not for sale to the public. Even if you wanted to buy them, you couldn't. They are simply IOUs from the Treasury to the Trust Funds. And even if the bonds were the types we know to be gold on the open market, they are debts the government owes to itself, payment of which can be deferred indefinitely. The only way to secure the funds would be to make them unavailable to the Congress by placing them under private management.

Surveys have shown over the past several years that the public likes the Social Security program, as the nation's basic retirement program; but the simple fact is that under the present structure we won't be able to sustain the program. Congress knows this but is unwilling to give up control of the system when it knows full well there are better, more efficient and cost-effective ways to run the system. Why are our lawmakers so stubborn? Because to recast Social Security means that Congress would also have to relinquish the power and influence it has derived from controlling the system.

Congress knows that the elderly support the program, that they want the benefits expanded, but do not want to pay more in taxes to avoid a reduction in Social Security benefits. That's asking a lot from government.

As we will see, there is a way, a very good way, to manage Social Security and give the average worker what he or she wants. Part III outlines the way to get the job done.

But first, let's get back to what has been going on. In 1994 the maximum amount of income from which FICA tax can be deducted was $60,600. That means the maximum an individual will pay into the Old-Age, Survivors and Disability Insurance (OASDI) portion of Social Security will be $3,757.20. The self-employed will pay almost twice that amount. That's a self-employed total of almost $7,514.40. Now that's a huge financial obligation no matter how you look at it. Every working man and woman is now paying two mandated taxes: an income tax used for all government operations, and a Social Security tax for retirement, which is our concern here.

At present, the retirement tax, called the Social Security tax by the government, is split into two parts: OASDI (the formal name for your retirement tax) receives 6.2 percent of the gross income of all employees, while an additional 1.45 percent is deducted to maintain old-age healthcare through Medicare. These payroll deductions total 7.65 percent, which comes out of your check whether you like it or not.

While this sounds very simple, it really isn't. All this money, together with the operations tax (income tax) simply goes into the Treasury to be used however Congress thinks best. Unlike a family budget, Congress doesn't put Social Security taxes into a separate account dedicated to the needs of the system. Instead, it takes note of the source of the funds (the paper Social Security Trust Funds) but pools the money with its general revenue, which Congress draws on to pay for the programs it passes. To further confuse things, lawmakers know that Medicare, as a separate healthcare obligation under Social Security, will go broke in several years. In order to prevent this mini crisis

Congress is already planning to shift funds from Social Security. It will be very interesting to see what this will do to Social Security's future. Perhaps jugglers should start running for Congress.

The 1994 Trustees' Report shows that within two decades the Social Security system will be due billions of dollars in interest alone on the nonnegotiable Treasury bonds it has been accumulating over the years. They may need every penny to meet these obligations. Two problems arise at this point. First, the trustees have no idea how much interest the funds are actually due. They estimate in various ways to show that this interest could be from $25 billion to $650 billion. Second, the trustees have no idea where the Treasury will come up with the money to pay this interest, let alone redeem the bonds. The only way Congress has ever paid interest is to issue more paper nonnegotiable bonds, and we now know how much they are worth.

In the past several years newspapers have come out with Op-Ed pieces that decry, "Get set America, for the coming bankruptcy of Social Security." These phantom funds will catch up with Congress in the not too distant future.

✱   ✱   ✱

There is a good example of how those elderly who are financially secure could help the system. If the 11.4 percent of the Social Security retirees now making over $50,000 per year were to refuse to take the Social Security checks they are now receiving, it would make a tremendous impact on the system. In fact it would return to Social Security over $50 billion per year. It would also stir the thinking of many people and remind this country of what President Kennedy said in his famous inaugural speech, "Ask not what the country can do for you, but what you can do for your country." True, some individuals actually do this right now, but the percentage is very small.

These phantom Social Security funds—the Treasury bond IOUs—evolved because we the people have allowed Congress to get away with it, simply because current beneficiaries are getting what they want and do not care about those who would need to collect benefits in the future.

This country became great because of the strength and drive of its people, not because of anything the government did. If any member of Congress understands this Rep. Bill Archer (R-Tex.) is a great example. He has been on the leading edge of the drive to recast Social Security. President Franklin D. Roosevelt, the leading Democrat of this era, also understood the dangers of institutions alleging a guaranteed government retirement plan. During his tenure he said,

> The lessons of history, confirmed by the evidence immediately before me show conclusively that continued dependence upon relief induces a spiritual and moral disintegration fundamentally destructive to the national fibre. To dole out relief in this way is to administer a narcotic, a subtle destroyer of the human spirit. It is inimical to the dictates of sound policy. It is in violation of the traditions of America.

The customer walked slowly up to the counter with the current issue of *Time* magazine. Twenty-eight-year-old Kathleen, assistant manager of the book store, could hardly contain herself. Kathleen's eyes lit up and she did a slow burn when the customer handed her the magazine.

As she took the magazine she looked at its cover "The Case for Killing Social Security." Her irate feelings could not be contained. "If I had anything to say about it," Kathleen muttered half-aloud, "I'd have shot it dead ten years ago when I came to work for the book store."

As she rang up the sale Kathleen continued her thinking and then spoke to the customer. "Those people in Congress sure have done us wrong," she said tersely. "They must really think we're dumb. They've run roughshod over us and then expect us to be happy about it. You work for forty years and if you are lucky you get about $900 per month from Social Security for all the money you've put into it. Big deal. The 401K plan that the book store offers to its employees is a much better way to handle your retirement. If I could opt out of Social Security, I sure would in a heart beat. I'd take the 6.2 percent I pay to Social Security and put it into the company 401K plan. That in addition to the funds the company puts into the plan would give me a real great retirement when I reach sixty-five. In fact, I could probably retire earlier. And to top it all off I could take the funds in the plan with me if I left the company."

"All Kathleen's co-workers feel the same way," said Michael, the book store manager. "This Social Security system has helped our folks, but how much will be left when we retire?"

As Kathleen gave the customer his change, she added, "All you have to do to see how people feel is to work in a bookstore for a month. You'll hear it all, and 95 percent want an independent system where their money can grow."

What worked many decades ago may not work very well today. In the private sector, chief executive officers of major corporations have found this out. If they don't keep pace with the times, their competitors pass them by. That is just the nature of things. Social Security is coming to a fork in the road, one that continues the same way of worries, increased taxes, and reduced benefits, or one that leads to a people-owned system that invests in profit-making vehicles and uses compound interest to augment the system's reserves. Which way it will go is anyone's guess. One thing is certain, it will not stay the same. Natural forces will never allow this. Members of Congress would do well to keep this in mind.

I have developed a concept that will bring Social Security into the twenty-first century in a way that will give everyone now and in the future an even chance to have a real retirement to look forward to— not with phantom promises, but with a system that is based on financial investment and sound rewards, a system that tells everyone how their retirement program is progressing and what's ahead for them.

7

The Independent Agency Question

"No country can long endure if its foundations are not laid deep in the material prosperity which grows, from thrift, from business energy and enterprise."

Theodore Roosevelt, 1899

Even though Social Security became an independent agency in the summer of 1994, and made the actual transfer to separate status on April 1, 1995, one question still remains. What is it independent from? This separate agency idea has been around since the 1970s, it's hardly new. In addition to the question of its status as a separate agency, Congress still had to determine exactly how much independence the agency should have.

Rep. Bill Archer (R-Tex.) and Rep. J. J. Pickle (D-Tex.) had tried for many years to sell Congress the idea of independent status for Social Security, but being in the minority on this issue they couldn't even get up to bat. With the shift in power after the 1994 Congressional elections things have now changed. The picture looks at least a little brighter for Social Security.

Finally after years of debating the idea of an independent Social Security Agency, Senator Moynihan (D-N.Y.), Chairman of the Senate Finance Committee (1994), saw a chance to pull it off and worked out a deal with the Clinton administration in exchange for voting for the Clinton budget that year. The deal went through and the Social Security Administration became a separate agency for the second time. What was gained from the deal? Did anyone benefit from this bureaucratic independence? At best all that can be said is that Social Security was removed from the jurisdiction of the Secretary of Health and Human Services. The severing of ties didn't benefit any recipients or reduce the cost of administering Social Security.

Is it any wonder that the work force as well as all retirees have grave doubts about what our government is doing? To millions of elders Social Security is the most important thing in their future. Yet it is frequently used as a pawn in political deal making. Such actions show how little politicians actually value this title transfer.

To the Washington bureaucrats an independent agency simply meant that Social Security was no longer an issue when lawmakers sit down to hammer out a budget for the fiscal year. But Social Security was never independent of government control or beyond Congress's power to spend and regulate. To most reasonable people this would be a very peculiar interpretation of independence.

Independence, in the true sense of the word, means self-governing, free from the larger governmental body. A good example is the Federal Reserve System, whose members are selected by the government but then function independently for specific terms. The Federal Reserve's goal is to watch money growth and interest rates adjusting both to maximize the level of economic growth. A truly independent Social Security system can only be accomplished by setting up a new, government-sponsored enterprise that will give this social retirement system back to the people it was designed to assist, the workers who for years gladly paid their share.

When President Roosevelt set up Social Security in 1935 it was established as an independent agency called the Social Security Board, managed by a three-member bipartisan panel. However, in 1939, the Social Security Board was placed under the Federal Security Agency (FSA), the forerunner of the Department of Health and Human Services. When this change was made the three-member panel was then replaced by a single commissioner.

For the first thirty years of its existence Social Security did a very good job of giving a helping hand to retirees, but then it started to outgrow itself. People lived longer, so benefits were increased without corresponding tax increases. In addition, larger numbers of people were retiring. Rather than do any farsighted planning, Congress decided to do nothing: even in these early years, Social Security was a program that no one fooled with if it wasn't absolutely necessary.

Keeping to this philosophy Congress simply catered to the perceived needs of the elderly. Even years ago the older citizens were a formidable voting bloc that sought to protect its hard-earned rewards for a productive life. Mindful of the power of this group, Congress consistently increased benefits until in the early 1980s the system was flat broke. Congress had played the reelection game too long! Instead of exercising oversight and actually reviewing the system each year, our leaders on Capitol Hill kept passing increases in the cost of living adjustment. These COLAs were great for recipients, but they wreaked havoc on Social Security finances. Even governments can run out of money! Remember, other costly social programs such as Supplemental Security Income (SSI) and aid to families with dependent children (AFDC) are financed by budget appropriations and not from the Social Security taxes. The government has limited additional resources to draw upon in the event of a Social Security crisis.

Here we are in 1995, just seven years away from repeating the

1982 fiasco in which a temporary solution was enacted that could have very easily taken care of the baby boomer generation and the tremendous upswing in the benefits curve they would cause. But Congress had other ideas that year. Members thought they could hide the real increase in the national debt, brought on by recession and the cost of President Reagan's tax cut, by using the Trust Fund surpluses. But these precipitous actions eroded earlier efforts to stabilize Social Security and to create a solid funding source for the foreseeable future.

Living on the edge is something most working people want no part of when it comes to retirement. Congress still has not learned this hard fact of life. Congressional leaders should have known that in the long run it would have been much safer and more sensible to treat the Social Security surpluses as real investments and followed through with programs that would have added additional earned income to the system. That time frame has long since passed out of congressional hands, because in less than a decade the annual surplus will come to an end. Complicating the congressional woes in this regard is the fact that Americans have smartened up. More people than ever before are informed about retirement planning and feel capable of managing their own financial future. The vast majority would have cheered such reforms, and Congress would have had something to point at with pride, a solvent retirement system. That is no longer possible.

Now that we have an independent Social Security Agency, and Shirley S. Chater has been properly installed as its first commissioner, does this mean it is a separate entity? Does the agency have the power to set monthly payments to recipients? Can it set the rates the taxpayers will pay? Can it receive the funds instead of the Treasury? Finally, can it invest these funds as though it were an investment manager, or will it still have to sit by and watch all the FICA revenue, including any surplus, go to the U.S. Treasury in exchange for the Treasury's now famous IOUs? Or are all of these prerogatives still retained by Congress and the administration?

Here is another question to ponder. How will this new agency get Congress and the Treasury to redeem $3.1 trillion in government bonds in twenty years as estimated in the 1995 Trustees Report, Table lll.B3. And where will the government find the money to pay off this huge debt? True, the$3.1 trillion would not have to be paid back all in one year, but certainly a large part will be needed to fund recipient benefits within the next two decades.

There is one very compelling reason for the complete privatization of Social Security. Within the next several decades government IOUs held by Social Security will balloon to an amount larger than the assets of the federal government. With the assets of Social Security intertwined with those of the government, it may be hard to determine who is running whom. The government is having an increasingly hard time running itself now without the added burden of handling the retirement needs of the many additional millions of working men and women who will retire over the next several decades. A completely separate system will be essential by the turn of the century.

Since the early 1970s the proponents of the privatization of Social Security have wanted to insulate it from the everyday fiscal and operational policies of Congress and the administration. They have repeatedly said that Social Security policy should be based on retirement objectives, not on the fiscal conditions that the government finds itself in every so often, nor the whims and fancies of Congress. The concerns of critics have been joined by the declining confidence the public has shown toward the integrity and financial soundness of the Social Security system.

What is really needed is a government-sponsored enterprise that completely privatizes a new retirement system. This would also solve the problem of Congress borrowing from a separate entity it does not control. As Barry Goldwater recently said, "You can't run a business borrowing money, and I've run a business. We're going to get to the point where every cent of tax we collect, local, state and federal, won't be able to pay the interest on our debt. That's a dumb fix to be in." Thomas Jefferson and Benjamin Franklin both worried about government borrowing. They said that some day it would become our worst nightmare, and it is fast becoming just that.

Harry J. Figgie, Jr., Chairman of Figgie International, a Fortune 500 company, has warned very emphatically about government borrowing from its trust funds. In his book, *Bankruptcy 1995,* Figgie says that Congress is borrowing not only from the Social Security Trust Funds, but from every other fund, such as the highway trust fund. All of these funds are stuffed with Treasury IOUs. * The opposing argument, says Figgie, runs as follows: "Borrowing from the Social Security Trust Funds and other trust funds and pension funds to finance the deficit is okay, because it keeps interest rates low and limits our need to borrow from foreign countries."

According to Figgie, "It would be okay if there were any prospect that the U.S. government will be able to repay those loans when the Social Security and other trust funds, such as military, postal workers, and railroad retirement, need the money themselves to pay benefits and meet their own obligations. But where will the cash come from? Borrowing to meet today's expenses from moneys that were meant to be set aside for the future is a cruel trick." He ends by saying, "Entitlement programs may make good social policy, but they play havoc with fiscal policy."

Congress and the administration will have to learn, as we all have, to stop borrowing from all available sources. As a nation we can't keep consuming all our assets. We are long past the point of no return and it makes no sense to continue down this well-worn path to chaos and oblivion. Certainly setting up a successful Social Security program under a completely independent agency, free from any government interference, administered by professionals whose job it is to invest and manage money, would be a practical alterna-

---

*Harry J. Figgie, Jr., and Gerald J. Swanson, *Bankruptcy 1995: The Coming Collapse of America and How to Stop It* (New York: Little, Brown, and Company, 1992).

tive. And I will attempt to develop just such a program later in this volume. But first we should consider the arguments put forth over the years by those who opposed independence for Social Security.

Critics of an independent Social Security system have argued that Social Security can't be a separate entity, because it takes in too much revenue and spends too much money. In fact it does neither. In the name of Social Security the U.S. Treasury handles these functions even though Social Security has independent status. In its present form Social Security is by definition a federal social program, not a contractual pension system: it is subject to periodic Congressional evaluation along with other economic and social functions of the government.

It is further argued that in setting up Social Security as an independent agency the program would greatly weaken and fragment domestic policy making by the administration. But thus far no apparent deterioration of government policy making capabilities has occurred. Changes if any in the way Social Security is handled in the United States have been virtually nonexistent.

The fact is that Social Security is now more than a helping hand. It is a full-blown retirement system. Right or wrong, this is how millions of Americans think of it. Unfortunately, the program as currently administered lacks the financial muscle to do the job. Working people now feel that they have earned their retirement, since throughout the years FICA has been deducted from their paychecks and they have acquired vested rights that no one can take from them. But this is far from the truth. Congress can adjust benefits at any time, even after you have retired.

If Social Security were actually a welfare program such as SSI, then why all the subterfuge? Why use two taxes : FICA and the income tax? Why not one simple income tax to cover everything? All other programs are considered welfare pure and simple, and have nothing to do with retirement.

Former Social Security Commissioner Stanford Ross stated a

decade ago, "There is no higher priority on the domestic side of government than finding a place for a comprehensive retirement income policy focus that looks at all programs together and attempts to bring rationality to this area. Giving different benefits to different groups of our citizens without any rational basis for doing so cannot go on forever."

"Giving" is the key word in this statement. You may give welfare programs to different groups of people for different reasons, but you do not give Social Security to anyone. They have to earn it, and they do so by acquiescing to the withholding of FICA taxes as long as they work.

True, the early retirees in the forties got a better return on their investment, percentage wise, but they did invest in the system through FICA taxes for as long as they worked. The system has been changing over the years and the time is fast approaching for another big leap forward to bring Social Security up to date.

Paul Hewitt, vice president of the National Taxpayers Union Foundation, and a leading expert on entitlement reform, wrote in early 1994, "Indeed, we are at a propitious moment. There is mounting evidence, ranging from the 1992 election returns to trends in national opinion, that the public will support politicians with the courage to lead us out of the entitlement spending vortex." The National Taxpayers Union Foundation's July 1993 Survey of Retirement Confidence found that 62 percent of Americans over age twenty-five would rather see cuts in Social Security and Medicare than yet another tax increase.

It seems that Congressman Bill Archer, Chairman of the House Ways and Means Committee, which oversees Social Security, agrees with Paul Hewitt. Archer has moved the Senior Citizens Equity Act through his committee and shortly it will be on its way to a vote by the full House in April 1995. The bill calls for provisions that will help senior citizens. It provides for an increase to $30,000 from $11,280, the amount that individuals age sixty-five through sixty-

nine can earn without having their Social Security payments reduced. It also looks forward by repealing the higher FICA taxes that
were voted in with the 1993 tax package. This act is a great step in
the right direction. It will be a strong indication that Congress is beginning to take note that things will have to change. Regressive
taxes may yet become a thing of the past.

In spite of Rep. Archer's good intentions, the black hole that Social Security now finds itself in has been too long in the making to
reverse the process in the usual Capitol Hill way. Only a completely
new retirement structure in another setting will get the job done. This
window of opportunity will not last long, but will be long enough if
everyone is sincere in finding a lasting solution.

Many so-called experts and economists promote the idea that retirement for most Americans stands on three legs like a trivet: Social
Security, pensions, and savings. Unfortunately, all of these programs
are on shaky ground these days, because of unforeseen population
growth and constant government interference. Let's take them in order.

Social Security in its present form is beyond help. Congress has
so gutted the system over the past fifteen years that there is basically
no way to replace the nearly one trillion dollars that will be needed
once the actual revenues start to exceed the outgo (benefits payments). The new Republican-controlled Congress will try valiantly,
but with its mind set on reducing taxes how will it acquire the necessary funds to fulfill the need. In other words how will it pay back
the money appropriated through the last fifteen years? The present
Congress will have to exercise a great deal of political courage to get
the job done.

Some people think that the government could just borrow more
money. But no amount of borrowing from existing sources will do
the job and even if it could be done, who would ultimately pick up
the tab? You and me, and every other American. What money the
government borrows it will ultimately have to repay. And those
payments will be with money collected through current taxes.

When the government goes into the credit markets to borrow money from existing sources to accumulate what it needs to maintain present benefits, it depletes some of the money available for home loans, personal borrowing, and corporate expansion. This makes money scare and drives interest rates up. Alternatively, the government could just print the money it needs to pay for retirement benefit claims. But if it pursues this route, then it risks flooding the economy with a mass of money, thereby potentially causing inflation and higher prices. Neither alternative is very attractive.

Pensions are the second part of this triumvirate. In the beginning when pensions were first developed it was a very good idea. But as the years went by and more and more workers reached retirement age the private sector began to feel the burden it had taken on. Some industries reached the point where they had more ex-workers in retirement than they did on their current payrolls. Realizing this the private sector began to change its thinking in order to survive. Lucrative benefit packages had to be shelved because corporate America could no longer support them. The costs were just too great. To remedy this situation investment firms started offering what were called 401K plans, which permitted the employee to invest part of his pay, a portion of which would be matched by the employer. Workers had to rethink their retirement. The money workers put into the 401K can be distributed among money market funds (short-term interest investments), fixed income investments (offering low risk but smaller returns), or stock investments (sometimes referred to as "equities" that offer higher interest but also are more risky). Statements show that most employees are conservative, staying with money markets or fixed income investments. Unfortunately, over time these investments don't do much better than outpacing inflation a bit.

Savings is the third leg of the triumvirate. It has been shown in poll after poll that this is the weakest part because less than 8 percent of working people can save a sufficient amount through the years to support themselves after retirement. This percentage goes down dramatically for those under age twenty-five, most of whom save less of their income.

Those who do save have found that the government tends to penalize them. When Individual Retirement Accounts (IRAs) were set up by Congress in 1984 to encourage savings, many taxpayers liked the idea and took advantage of it in a big way. When IRAs were first created an individual could save a total of $2,000 per year and deduct the amount from his or her taxable income. Families could deduct a total of $4,000 per year. Tax was to be taken when withdrawals were made at retirement, and interest on these savings accumulated tax deferred. So many people were putting so much money into IRAs that it began to cut into government revenues, so Congress, naturally, changed the rules. Limits were placed on the tax advantages of IRA contributions, and to no one's surprise savings dropped. Employees earning less than $25,000 can still contribute up to $2,000 per year and have that amount fully tax deductible from their gross income. But for every $1,000 a person earns over $25,000 the tax deductible portion of the contribution drops by $200. Is it any wonder that this trivet is on shaky ground? Who can tell what Congress will come up with next year?

Two couples were having dinner together at a nice restaurant. During the conversation Chuck said to Dave, "Sarah and I would like to start saving for our future but it is so hard. I guess we will have to depend on Social Security for a big chunk of our retirement." When asked by Dave how much he knew about Social Security, Chuck said, "I've been told that the money they take out of my pay each week is invested by the government so we'll have a good retirement."

Dave explained that that wasn't the way Social Security works. The government simply takes your money and pays all the current retirees; if there is anything left, it spends the money on anything it wants. When you retire in thirty years your benefits will depend upon how many workers are putting money into the system at the time you retire. The best thing for you to do is put twenty dollars per week into savings. When you retire at least you will have something to take care of you. You'd be surprised at how much.

Such conversations take place throughout the country. There are over 129 million working people in America and in 1995 more than 75 percent had thoughts similar to those Chuck expressed. For many of these young people the few thoughts they might have about retirement are eclipsed by concerns about finding a good job, buying the nice things that make life meaningful, possibly marriage and children and all that goes with it. Few realize that they would have to start at nearly age twenty-five to have a top-notch retirement forty years later.

Most Americans want to trust their institutions and government, but when the time comes to receive those benefits circumstances sometimes change. It's not quite what they expected. Recently AARP Vice President Joe Perkins said Social Security is sound for the foreseeable future. He then added that some changes are needed to maintain the program's long-term solvency and that if decisions are made soon they will be less painful than if corrective action is delayed. Well, Mr. Perkins, is Social Security sound or isn't it?

Did the fact that Congress made Social Security a separate agency do anything to help? As we've seen, it might have been a very small step in the right direction. But we have a *long* way to go.

"There is no cause so sacred as the cause of a people. There is no idea so uplifting as the idea of service to humanity."

Woodrow Wilson, 1912

PART TWO

The Colossal Private Pension Debacle

8

A Short History of Pension Plans

"Public virtue is the vital spirit of republics, and history proves that when this has decayed and the love of money has usurped its place, although the forms of free government may remain for a season, the substance has departed forever."

James Buchanan, 1857

The rash of corporate takeovers that has occurred over the past two decades was brought about for many reasons, among them corporate survival tinged with a bit of greed. In any case, it was done at the expense of thousands of workers' jobs as corporations consolidated their work forces. These mergers also had an effect on many of the private pension plans. Take, for example, Chevron Oil Company's buyout of Gulf Oil Company in the mid 1980s.

Some forty thousand Gulf Oil workers had to file a class action suit against Chevron in order to get their full pension benefits.* In November of 1990, the Gulf Oil workers received a $25 million partial settlement for their claims. They were seeking an additional $600 million dollars in retirement benefits to compensate them for not being given the pension and severance payments promised to them after the merger. Workers claimed that their benefits were reduced when Chevron took over the Gulf Oil pension and retirement program funds and joined them in a separate plan two years after the companies merged. In October 1994, the 5th Circuit Court of Appeals told the former Gulf Oil employees they had no claim. It was Chevron's money. It will now be up to the U.S. Supreme Court. Who was right and who was wrong is not the issue here (though the case is an important one). The real point is this: Under a retirement system independent of the company this would never have happened and both the employer and employees would be satisfied.

In another case thousands of J.C. Penney workers will share in up to $80 million through a settlement approved in a federal lawsuit over the company's former method for determining pensions. In February 1995, U.S. District Judge Joe Kendall signed an order approving the class action settlement in which individual members, including both present and former employees, could receive several thousand dollars apiece. This was a major victory for well over thirty thousand J.C. Penney employees, most of them women, who previously received little or no pension from Penney's after years of labor. The company had used a formula that subtracted estimated Social Security benefits from the pension. Using such calculations, some employees received nothing.

The company arbitrarily assumed that employees had been paying into the Social Security system since age twenty-two. For some of its employees, the job at Penney's was their first and they didn't start working until their children were grown. This presumption negatively affected the employees' benefits.

*Houston Post, November 1, 1990.

Then there is the case of the sexton who had worked for a New England church for over twenty years and was close to retirement. He had outlasted several ministers and many lay people. Even though the church is well endowed for this purpose, the sexton has had to spend the past two years negotiating his retirement plan because new lay people who run the church finances have shown very little concern for fairness. The sexton may have to take the church to court to receive the pension promised to him in writing many years ago.

Each of these cases points to the fact that retirement plans are getting out of hand for any number of reasons, but the principal one seems to be that pension plans are now beginning to become a financial burden on the companies, corporations, and businesses that started them in good faith years earlier. When the cost of maintaining the pensions overloaded corporate financial obligations, some firms chose to underfund their retirement plans rather than go belly up.

These cases all could have been avoided if an independent retirement system had been in place.

If you think the cases cited are isolated incidents, then just look at what is going on today throughout industry and government. In the private sector General Motors has the dubious distinction of having the number one underfunded pension plan. They were at the $20 billion dollar underfunded mark in 1994 according to the 1994 Pension Benefit Guaranty Corporation annual report,* and who knows where they will go from there. And yet the company has not done this on its own. The unions must assume their share of the blame, through constant demands for higher pensions regardless of GM's huge underfunding. No one seems to know when enough is enough. This liability could someday bring down this top notch auto maker.

The underfunding of the top fifty U.S. companies with pension problems has grown ever larger. In 1994 alone the level at which

---

*Much like the Federal Deposit Insurance Corporation (FDIC) that insures savings deposits, the Pension Benefit Guarantee Corporation (PBGC) safeguards the pension system through contributions by its corporate participants.

they are underfunded has increased by over $1.7 billion, according to the listings put out by the Pension Benefit Guaranty Corporation (PBGC)! The next chapter will detail these problems.

Together the fifty state governments have underfunded their pension plans to the tune of approximately $230 billion, while the U.S. government has come up short in its various pension systems by over $1 trillion dollars! If you think it's hard to balance the budget now, in both the state and federal governments, just wait till these liabilities start to come due several decades down the line.

Underfunding simply means that a company or a government (either federal, state, or local), in order to get more production out of their employees, has made some very nice promises about what will done when their workers reach retirement age. Employers have often made these promises of lucrative pensions and benefits without having any good idea how to come up with the money to pay for them, that is, without breaking the backs of a lot of working people. Each year corporate or public officials who find themselves in a fiscal bind choose to put off that year's pension funding to make the company look better for the stockholders or to make the government's budget balance. But one day they find that the pension obligations so far out-of-kilter that the company or government either goes under from the load, or a restructuring is required that costs many people their jobs. In many cases it's the employees who are shoved out in the cold. Often it's easier to let existing pension plans take the biggest hit by reducing monthly benefits to cover the plan's obligations. In most cases a company doesn't do this out of spite, but to stay alive and keep from drowning in a sea of red ink. The steel industry of twenty five years ago is a great example of this type of problem.

The previously mentioned case of General Motors is another classic example. It underfunded its pension plan for so many years that it is now some $20 billion behind in payments to the fund. And this is in spite of the fact the GM contributed $4 billion in cash and stock to its pension trust in 1993. Part of the problem is the fact that, in the same year, the plan was increased by $2 billion to reflect mainly the richer benefits granted to the United Auto Workers Union in their new contract. Who is really thinking of the future in this case? Both GM and the unions may very well "kill the goose that lays the golden egg" with this type of agreement.

The employees must also assume their share of the blame for what may happen to General Motors in the future. They approved this huge new pension obligation when they ratified the union contract with management. There is an old saying, "Everything in moderation," but in America these days few seem to want to hold to this standard. Then, too, there are no saints in many executive suites. They make sure they are well taken care of with their multimillion dollar salaries, bonuses, and golden parachutes.* When they come up with less than great decisions and the company loses money, their financial reward should reflect their poor judgment.

General Motors is not the only big corporation trying to shore up its pension plans by using corporate stock or stock from its subsidiaries rather than cash to fund its retirement system. Others include companies such as PPG Industries, Tenneco, Chrysler, Cummins Engine Co., Cargill Inc. and Penn Central, to name a few. For the most part they all do this for one simple reason; they are cash poor. But the Pension Benefits Guaranty Corporation (PBGC) is now demanding that corporations bring their pension plans up to date by eliminating their underfunding. The net worth of General Motors in 1994, after several bad years, was only some $6 billion plus. In 1995 it has returned to profitability. In the long run it is hoped GM will solve its problems, but only time will tell.

Recently the Securities and Exchange Commission (SEC) has been causing concern in corporate America by telling all companies

---

*Golden parachutes are agreements made by corporate executives to provide them with a financial soft landing if they leave the corporation for any reason. The agreements may include cash payments, stock options, and other forms of compensation.

that accounting practices will have to change to conform with today's standards. They are getting tough by insisting that accounting procedures used to report the financial soundness of retirement plans should better reflect the current lower interest rate climate. By lowering the discount rate one percentage point the Federal Reserve can increase a company's pension liability from between 10 and 15 percent. The discount rate is the rate that business is charged for borrowing. Some pension managers may play with these figures by calculating the return on their invested funds at higher interest rates, thus making the funds appear more sound than they are. Management may know it can't come up with the cash needed to fund its pension, but rather than be up front with the employees it does its best to play the numbers game to satisfy all concerned. Just another reason for a new independent retirement system.

When it comes to the federal government, Congress believes in putting off until next year what it can get away without financing this year. Our lawmakers in Washington seem always to be thinking that it's okay to make all sorts of promises, because as legislators they won't be around when dues paying time comes along anyway.

Whether we like it or not the American people are sometimes as much to blame as those in Congress. Instead of holding our congressmen's collective feet to the fire, when our representatives get out of line we let the government do as it pleases, just as long, of course, as our particular group gets what it thinks it's entitled to.

Many great and good ideas began with admirable intentions but have outlived their usefulness and are in desperate need of modification. A television program recently studied the cases of two welfare families. Both families had parents who were fully capable of working, but found it a great deal easier to justify staying on welfare. All of the parents got in trouble in their teen years and are now paying the price. And when the gray hair starts to show they'll wonder why they have nothing to look forward to. It's simply because they were feeling sorry for themselves and wouldn't stand on their feet

and make a life for themselves and their families. Hard, rough. Sure
it will be, but you only have one chance at life, so why not give it a
try. That's the kind of inspiration to give to your children. In part 3
we will see how a busboy or server will have a sound retirement
under this new system. It can be done.

The Tennessee Valley Authority (TVA), as we all know, did a
great job for the Tennessee Valley and surrounding states for many
decades, by building a network of dams that brought electricity and
prosperity to this area of the country. However, the day has come
when it no longer serves the purpose it was designed for, and now
only benefits a few at a high price to everyone. The Department of
Agriculture is in the same boat. There are almost as many people
working in the department as there are farmers. In addition the department handles the food stamp program, but for what reason?
True, farmers grow all the crops, but what does that have to do with
issuing food stamps to people who are down on their luck?

Since the advent of the Industrial Revolution in the nineteenth century, the labor market has grown more sophisticated and better educated. Private-sector companies realized that they needed additional
inducements to retain top-notch employees. This led to the early beginnings of pension and retirement plans. Thus the retirement move-
ment in the United States is rooted in the social and economic development of the twentieth century. One of the most pressing economic
problems throughout this century has been settling upon the best way
to provide a measure of financial security for the aged.

Private pension plans date back to late in the nineteenth century.
The first such pension plan was originated by the American Express
Company in 1875. Earlier, in 1867, the American Express and
United States Express Companies organized the Expressman's Mu-
tual Benefit Association, which set up a fund from which payments

would be made to families of deceased employees. These two companies were some of the first to provide delivery services for parcels throughout the United States, using the railroads as the primary source of transportation.

At the executive committee meeting of American Express on November 16, 1875, chaired by President William G. Fargo, and attended by other committee members, Theodore M. Pomeroy, First Vice President, and Alexander Holland, Treasurer, it was resolved to set up a "Pension Account" to provide assistance to employees of the company who were "injured or worn out in the service." These colorful terms come straight from the 1867 records of their meetings. This marked the beginning of pension plans by private companies in the United States.

An extract from the executive committee meeting of March 28, 1876, reads as follows:

> The committee on the recommendation of the Gen'l Supt. authorized the payment of pensions to old and disabled employees as per list below, to commence 1st April 1876 and continue during the pleasure of the board.
>
> C.H. Hearst for many years a Messenger and Agent at St. Thomas, Ont. to be allowed $25 per month.
>
> Geo. Wheeler an old Messenger $25 per Mo.
>
> Jno. H. Parsons for many years a clerk in Buffalo Office $41.66 per Mo.
>
> A. Rogers an extra Messenger at Buffalo $41.67 per Mo.
>
> and such names as may be found reported by Asst. Gen'l and Div'n Supts, that the Gen'l Supt may decide to be worthy. The maximum allowance not to exceed $500 per annum, nor more than half pay.

Then an extract from the records of the meeting on April 21, 1876 reads:

In pursuance of the authority given him be the Committee at the last meeting the Gen'l Supt reported that he had placed the following additional names upon the Pension List, viz:

J.T. Lacey, Buffalo	to draw $41.67 per Mo.
J.T. Boniface, Detroit	" " 33.75 " "
J.W. Taylor, Kalamazoo	" " 41.67 " "
W.S. Brown, Chicago	" " 37.50 " "

all to commence Apl 1, 1876.

By 1900 American Express had paid $653,074 to pensioners in the first twenty-five years of the pension plan. From that point on the pension plan took on definite characteristics. The plan became permanent and set out guidelines as to age and years of service. In 1973 vesting was incorporated into the plan as well as early retirement. The plan continued to grow to stay in touch with the times.

This pension plan idea and its implementation demonstrated the wisdom and foresight of these early executives of American Express. The plans that followed for the American Express Company used this initial effort as an example and officials continued their thinking and understood the right way to run a company.*

The Baltimore and Ohio Railroad saw the effects on key workers and formally adopted America's second major retirement plan in 1880. From that time on the pension plan idea grew throughout corporate America. Many unions in those early days, in particular the United Mine Workers, saw the advantages of such plans and pushed for better pensions and more benefits during the decades that followed.

---

*This information was generously furnished by Mr. Whitney Blair, Archives, American Express Company, World Financial Center, New York. Excerpts are taken directly from copies of actual 1893 records.

A decade later, the pension plan idea really took hold. In 1899 the Pennsylvania Railroad followed in the Baltimore and Ohio's footsteps and established a pension plan for its employees that would later become the model plan for the early twentieth century. In 1900, the Chicago North Western Railway put in a pension system, which was soon followed by the Illinois Central Railway Company. The Pennsylvania Railroad pension covered all railroad workers and no employee was ever required to contribute to the plan. Retirement was compulsory at the age of seventy. There was just one stipulation: the worker had to have thirty years of service in order to qualify for a pension. By 1910 most of the largest railroads throughout the country had seen the wisdom of such a plan and followed the lead of the Pennsylvania Railroad by starting similar pension plans for their workers.

In the first four decades of the new century, hundreds of multifaceted companies signed on to similar retirement plans as pensions spread throughout the private sector. Public utilities, banking, and manufacturing took the lead. Dupont had developed its retirement plan and had it in place by 1910. Just one year later U.S. Steel started one. Many others then followed suit.

In the early boom years with a fairly young work force and few retirees, the plans flourished. But the years rolled by and cyclical ups and downs occurred in business as the number of retired employees grew along with the pension liabilities for the companies involved. The long-range picture was beginning to change. Pensions became a permanent expense on corporate profit and loss statements, and companies began to wonder what they had gotten themselves into. That's when they began to think about defined-contribution plans and the idea of using Social Security to reduce their exposure.

In 1920 there were some five million workers who had reached the age sixty-five. Fifty years later there were over 24.4 million people of retirement age. By the turn of the twenty-first century this figure will top out at over sixty million, as the Baby Boomer generation starts to retire. World War II had a great many long-lasting effects on this country, and this dynamic Baby Boomer generation is one outstanding example.

In 1930 there were some 2.8 million workers covered by pension plans valued at $800 million. By 1964 this had increased to 27.7 million workers covered, with over $76.2 billion in assets. Today these plans total in the trillions of dollars and are growing every year.

Today in the nineties we are seeing the culmination of nearly a hundred years in the growth of pension plans. Oddly enough they have been tracking the same torturous path that Social Security has been following. Through the years corporate down-sizing has been the rule as large, often multinational companies seek to improve their financial picture for stockholders.

Republic Steel of a few decades ago was a classic example of problems of a pension fund. Badly underfunded to begin with (it had $275 million in assets to cover $625 million in funding liabilities) the executives of the corporation had set the fund up so that anyone could retire and take lump sum payouts. In a short period of time those executives had taken most of the available funds out of the plan through lump sums at retirement. The LTV Corporation later absorbed Republic Steel only to repeat the early retirement of executives, thus depleting pension reserves while the employees' retirement went right down the drain.

Perhaps a better title to this chapter would be "Imperiled Promises." Since pensions were started by the American Express Company back in 1875, businesses have been, in many cases, promising more than they can or will deliver, and the government has been letting them get away with it for too long. True, nearly 85 percent of all pension plans are sound today, but the other 15 percent are not only hurting themselves and their retirees, but also putting a strain on all working people through increased taxation to handle their problems through the Pension Benefit Guaranty Corporation, through unemployment compensation, and many other welfare programs.

Congress has come very close to destroying the entire group of retirement systems it has so carefully developed over the years through its thoughtless actions in the recent past. Only by implementing a completely new system will we be free of governmental intervention. These problems can be solved, make no mistake about it. It just takes dedication and a willingness to do what is right.

"The business of government is not directly to make people rich, but to protect them in making themselves rich; and a government which attempts more than this is precisely the government which is likely to perform less. Governments do not and cannot support the people."

Thomas Macaulay, 1831

9

The Pension Benefit
Guaranty Corporation

"We should never despair, our situation before has been un-
promising and has changed for the better, so I trust, it will happen
again. If new difficulties arise, we must only put forth New Exer-
tions and proportion our efforts to the exigency of the times."

George Washington, 1777

When this country started out on its own, some two hundred years
ago, people for the most part lived and worked on the East Coast,
from New England to Georgia. When things were not good, whole
families turned their eyes west and thought of new beginnings, new
lands and opportunities. They were strong and self-reliant, and with
this kind of spirit brought us through the maturing experiences of the
past two hundred years to the mighty country we are today.

The federal government encouraged this great growth and expansion, and gave these sturdy and far-sighted pioneers of this by-

gone era the opportunity to settle this great and wonderful land. The West was opened and the country grew from one coast to the other. In the West, from the Mississippi River to the Rockies and beyond, farming and ranching became a way of life. The plains became the bread basket for the country and later on for the world. The opportunities seemed endless. With the coming of the transcontinental railroads the entire country flourished.

But this era of looking West for new opportunities soon passed and by World War I the land to the west was no longer a golden opportunity. The Industrial Revolution had firmly established itself and workers had to look in a different direction for their future. This was the sweat and muscle generation, that held on through the first part of the twentieth century. Day after day, for ten to twelve hours at a time, workers labored in long assembly lines putting together the various parts to make cars, tractors, vacuum cleaners, and other mass-produced items. Pensions and retirement was the last thing on their minds. First they had to get through today.

With the outbreak of World War II the private sector promised workers all sorts of perks, including pension plans, to keep the best workers. In the 1940s, John L. Lewis, President of the United Mine Workers Union, saw what pensions could do for the coal miners and through his efforts they were one of the first unions to win pensions for the workers. True, they more than earned the pensions, but no one really looked to the future to see where this idea, no matter how good it may have been, was taking the companies, the unions, and the workers.

As we've learned, pensions were born long before this era, but until the post-World War II period there were virtually no controls over how these retirement systems were run or administered. In many cases management played fast and loose with pension promises and never gave their fulfillment a second thought. With the advent of the Social Security System in 1935 business found another way to avoid paying the full amount it had promised workers. Employers just deducted the Social Security benefits a worker was entitled to at age sixty-five from the amount their pensions would pay. It wasn't until much later that the government finally enacted laws, such as the Employee Retirement Income Security Act of 1974, that would put a stop to this shabby practice.

The Pension Benefit Guaranty Corporation (PBGC) came about because of several major incidents in the early 1960s and 1970s. As J. J. Pickle (D-Tex.), Chairman of the Subcommittee on Oversight said in a hearing held in 1992, "In 1963, the conscience of the American public was shocked by the failure of the Studebaker pension plan. People who had worked for Studebaker for over thirty years found themselves destitute because the Studebaker pension plan had almost no assets. It was nothing but an empty promise, a fraud on the worker. The public was outraged and demanded federal action."*

It wasn't to come though, for another ten years after the Studebaker tragedy. The final straw came in 1971 when the Raybestos-Manhattan Company closed its plant in Passaic, New Jersey, leaving all the workers holding the bag for uncollectible pensions and other promises the company made. This really riled the unions, which persuaded the state's U.S. Senator, Harrison A. Williams, Jr., chairman of the Senate Labor Committee, to look into a bill for federal pension guarantees. The result of all this was that Congress passed the Employee Retirement Income Security Act of 1974 (ERISA). A key goal of ERISA was to promote retirement security by requiring that pension plans be fully funded and by guaranteeing that certain benefits would be paid by the federal government even if the company pension plan failed before it was properly funded.

The federal government's Pension Benefit Guaranty Corporation now picks up the tab, within certain limitations, if it has been insuring the company whose pension goes under. The PBGC is the government agency that insures and polices the private pension plans of this country. They have been doing a good job, but the state of some

---

*Studebaker was for years one of America's leading independent automobile manufacturers.

current pension plans has reached the point where the benefit commitments are more then they can handle.

The problem lies with companies that have made some very questionable promises, have underfunded their pension plans, and have no thought of ever fully funding these plans. In some cases it is doubtful that the companies have the resources to fund their plans and still stay in business.

Congress did little to stop this because the principle of sound pension funding was largely ignored since ERISA had minimum funding rules. Unfortunately, these rules were neither specific enough nor adequately enforced, which made it all too easy for employers to get around them. In recent years Congress has been tightening up the rules, and changes are now being made. Under the new pension reforms, companies whose plans are less than 90 percent funded will be required to provide workers and retirees with annual, easy-to-understand explanations of the plan's funding status, according to a PBGC news release dated December 13, 1994.

Every year the Pension Benefit Guaranty Corporation, set up under ERISA, puts out a list of the top fifty problem companies. The latest list was released on December 13, 1994, and showed that the total underfunding increased from $38 billion in 1993 to $39.733 billion in 1994. The top ten companies with underfunded liabilities are:

General Motors	$19.447	billion
LTV Corporation	2.190	billion
Westinghouse Electric	2.046	billion
Bethlehem Steel	1.943	billion
Navistar International	914	million
United Technologies	799	million
ACF Industries/TWA	689	million
Northwest Airlines	647	million
US Air Group	573	million
Uniroyal Goodrich Tire	$ 532	million

This list firmly underscores the need for further pension funding reforms and provides additional evidence that current law is still not working as well as it can. There were other bills before Congress to aid and help improve these conditions. Will the new Republican Congress do the job? Only time will tell. What it shows is that another solution is needed to get the job done, and without adding further to the financial load already shouldered by the taxpayer.

For the most part this underfunding by so many companies shows that the age of pension funding has seen its glory days. Companies simply cannot maintain an expense that is never ending and always growing.

Although retirement is one of the things uppermost in the mind of any middle-aged or older worker these days, less than 10 percent of these employees have put aside enough to take care of themselves when they retire. Everyone has come to believe that Social Security or private company sponsored retirement plans will do the job, but the elderly know it isn't so. You just cannot live on the small benefits program from Social Security or private pension plans. Why do you think the elderly keep asking for cost of living increases to keep them ahead of inflation, and stood up to cheer when Congress enacted the annual COLA program into law? It is good for the elderly, but the rest of America's work force will pay dearly for the decision. Recently a number of senators have called for an investigation into how the Consumer Price Index (CPI) is adjusted. This is the list of goods and services the price changes which result in the rate of increase for COLAs.

The only way to take care of this continuing problem is to set up a system that will adapt to changing circumstances without increasing income taxes or payroll deductions for FICA. We need programs that will not continue to heap burdens on business and government.

Without a doubt the Pension Benefit Guaranty Corporation (PBGC) has helped to preserve and protect private sector pensions. A good example of this is Pan American World Airways. During its high-flying, glory years its planes flew the globe and its pilots made in excess of $125,000 per year. Other employees made comparatively high salaries. But salaries and benefits cannot continue to rise forever and an airline cannot stay competitive when its costs escalate so rapidly. Where would this Pam Am odyssey end? Just where it did—in bankruptcy court with all the creditors picking over the corporate bones. After its demise the company still had pension liabilities of over $700 million. In October 1994, the PBGC, which inherited this pension debt, had to settle for $115 million from bankruptcy proceeds. This will help pay benefits to thirty-seven thousand former employees in the Pan American pension plans. How did the former employees fare? Most received up to $1,058 a month, the maximum payable by PBGC under law, but at this rate several thousand pilots and flight engineers received only half of what was coming to them under the pension plans.

Since its inception under Title IV of the Employee Retirement Income Security Act in 1974, the Pension Benefit Guaranty Corporation has done a very good job with the tools it was given. Today there are some 41 million workers participating in approximately 66,000 pension plans administered by the PBGC, according to PBGC's Newsletter of December 13, 1994.

In addition, the PBGC currently pays monthly retirement benefits to about 145,000 retirees in about 1,700 terminated plans. More than 200,000 workers will be paid benefits when they reach retirement age, based on their terminated pension plan, up to the maximum as provided by law. The PBGC has also become the trustee of one of the largest pension plans in its history as the airline industry fell on hard times. More than 80,000 participants are relying on the PBGC for their pensions since Eastern Airlines joined its sister air carrier Pan American World Airways in filing for bankruptcy and passed on into the annals of airline history.

These air carriers were not the first or only airlines to go this route. Back in 1982, when Braniff International went bankrupt, the same thing happened. Thousands of airline workers were grateful that the PBGC was in place to protect their pensions. Today the PBGC can look forward to having another 250,000 retirees added to its programs when they reach retirement age.

Today pension underfunding has its biggest problems in the auto, steel, airline, and tire and rubber industries. The auto industry accounts for almost 55 percent of the underfunding of the listed companies. Farther on down the line the steel industry has approximately $7 billion in underfunded pensions; the airlines are groping for over $2 billion for the same reason, and the tire and rubber industries have got a $1.2 billion headache.

These companies and others like them will have an increasingly difficult time surviving in the current market place because of additional financial burdens that in no way produce a profit for the corporations involved.

Remember, just because a company is on the PBGC list does not mean that an employee's benefits are in jeopardy. It simply represents a financial exposure that the PBGC must monitor. Although a majority of retirees are fully covered if their plan has to be taken over by the insurance fund, there are limits to PBGC's guarantee. Under the new pension reforms, companies whose plans are less than 90 percent funded will be required to provide workers and retirees with an annual report that tells the plan's funding status and the limits of PBGC's guarantee.

The need for these reforms exposes a lot of questionable promises made by many companies, most of them made with the best of intentions, but one wonders if these companies are now taking advantage of the PBGC. Many in Congress and in the administration are considering strengthening the PBGC even more, especially in light of the savings and loan bailouts of the 1980s. But while such a move may be needed, is it the real solution? Maybe other ideas should be looked at. The retirement business has reached the point where the pension load a business must carry to satisfy its obligations to workers is completely out of proportion to the company's size or its ability to meet those obligations.

The Pension Benefit Guaranty Corporation is financed through premiums collected from companies that sponsor insured pension plans, investment returns on PBGC assets, and recoveries from employers responsible for underfunded and terminated plans. Premiums for the insurance program are paid annually by plan administrators or employers. Premiums for the insurance program originally started at a one-dollar flat rate per participant, but have now reached $19 per participant, plus additional variable rates depending on several other factors. But like every other tax (and it really is a tax because it is assessed by a government agency), regression sets in when it goes too high. When the costs of participating become too great many good companies pull out of the program to find less expensive private solutions to their pension needs.

Can a reasonable balance ever be reached? It's a dilemma not unlike the problems with Social Security. Many companies have simply changed from a defined-benefit retirement plan (through which your employer promises you a lifetime pension benefit) to a defined-contribution pension (to which your employer makes an annual contribution, but makes no promises about the final amount of your retirement benefit) or a thrift plan in which the employee does his or her own investing. The PBGC does not insure either of the last two plans. Then of course there is the problem of not knowing what will happen in the years ahead as the tax laws change and the deductibility of employer and employee contributions alters according to Congressional whim. Congress has gotten itself in so deep over the years in its effort to please various interest groups that it has to keep looking for new sources of revenues (goods, services, or people to tax). Recall what happened to the Individual Retirement Accounts Congress created to inspire saving. Once people started putting two thousand dollars per year per individual into the program and in so doing reaping the savings and tax benefits from them, the government saw its tax base go down, so it changed the rules, leaving many Americans feeling betrayed.

The Annual Report of the PBGC for 1991 projected losses over a ten year period. It is estimated that these losses will run to over $18 billion by the turn of the century. It is good to know that the PBGC exists to handle these problems, but better yet, economic and legal incentives should be created to fund pensions and eliminate many of the hazards and problems. Money is not always the answer.

In November or December of each year the PBGC puts out a recap of the problems in private sector pension plans during the previous year. The report is distributed to most government officials, while many newspapers and magazines also request copies. Any citizen can get a copy by requesting it from the PBGC. But oddly enough, until very recently the employees of the top fifty problem companies would not have known that their pensions were in any serious trouble. New government regulations have rectified this. The employees now have to be notified by their company if their pension plan has been listed as a problem plan. With this knowledge workers can better plan for their future retirement.

Even the stockholders of these companies have the opportunity to know about the corporation's pension problems if they take the time to read the annual reports they receive. Of course, few actually do, since these reports are often viewed as an incomprehensible propaganda pieces put out by the company. But investors should learn. There is a wealth of information hidden among all the back slapping and picture taking.

In 1993 twelve companies made PBGC's dubious hit list. In 1994 another thirteen companies made the list of doubtful distinction, while several companies tried very hard, increased their pension contributions, and were removed. For all the employees of Chrysler Corporation and Deere & Company it's nice to hear, but what effect did it have on these companies and their profitability? Time will make this known.

The thirteen new companies to make the PBGC list published on December 13, 1994, were:

US Air Group	$573*
National Steel	448
Kaiser Aluminum	352
AK Steel Corporation	296
United Parcel Service	295
Loral Corporation	292
Baxter International	264
Textron Inc.	210
Borden	153
Nestle USA Inc.	147
Teamsters Affiliates Pension Plan	128
Cooper Industries	116
Foxboro	$109

*The amounts listed are in millions

The additions are from many different industries, which indicates that the pension crunch is being felt throughout the private sector.

There is yet one more problem with the private pension system in the United States: under current law employers can minimize their contributions by using more optimistic retirement age, mortality, and interest rate assumptions, given the current flexibility in the law. For example, mortality rates today say that the average person will live 15.5 years after retiring at age sixty-five. However, further research by the Congressional Research Service shows that over 65 percent of those now retired will outlive this assumption. Then too, if the interest rate used is higher than the current market rates, it will show greater anticipated income.

The 1993 news release of PBGC suggests that to bring these problems under control much more attention should be given to writing better guidelines. The Securities and Exchange Commission, the government agency that regulates the country's stock and bond markets, in 1993 recommended to the Financial Accounting Standards Board that companies use more current interest rates to value their pension liabilities. In that way they will be closer to those used by PBGC in determining the same pension liabilities. PBGC's reforms specify the interest rates and mortality assumptions to be used in determining private pension contributions.

The administration's reforms, covered by the Retirement Protection Act of 1993, had been introduced as bill HR3396 by Representative William D. Ford. There were several good things about this act. It strengthened funding rules, enhanced PBGC's compliance authority, raised premiums on the worst cases, and required companies with underfunded plans to provide workers and retirees with easy-to-understand information on the plans' funding status.

The Board of Directors of the PBGC consists of the secretaries of the departments of labor, treasury, and commerce, with the secretary of labor serving as the chair. They also have a seven member advisory committee. These are the officials responsible for letting the public in on this open secret. However, it may be hard to do, considering that the board has met so few times since PBGC's inception. Perhaps the time has come to consider a nongovernmental board that will have the time to give serious attention to the problems of the PBGC.

The problems surrounding retirement in the United States continue to mount because of the sheer numbers of those currently retired and those who are about to claim benefits. The government cannot possibly see to the needs of all these people. The current systems both public and private have performed well for decades, but their days are numbered because of the continuing growth in the sheer numbers of benefit recipients. The numbers show pension growth in its present form will continue to expand for the next several decades.

In August and September 1992, the House Congressional Subcommittee on Oversight conducted hearings to review the financial condition of the Pension Benefit Guaranty Corporation and to consider proposals for reducing the growth in federal contingent liabilities. As then Chairman J. J. Pickle (D-Tex.), put it, "In recent years, despite reforms adopted, significant numbers of large and severely underfunded pension plans have either terminated or failed to improve their financial condition. This has resulted in a significant increase in the future liabilities (some $40 billion currently) of the PBGC." Billions of dollars are at stake yet the general public and the workers in many of these pension plans know little if anything about it. How will these dedicated people feel when they request their pensions only to find they may not get anywhere near the amounts promised? A quote by Chairman Pickle summed up the committee's thinking on these problems. "It is important that we give serious attention to proposals which limit the exposure of the federal government to tens of billions of dollars in unfunded pension liabilities."

Ours is a country of individual initiative, and we should not look to Washington every time something goes wrong. One great way to encourage this initiative is to take retirement out of the hands of the government and put it where it belongs, in the hands of the people.

We must look to an independent system that has no other job than to see that all workers receive a sound pension, one that will relieve them of any worries when they retire. That, and only that, is what we should aspire to when we set our sights on a sound retirement system.

The government with all of its programs, and the private sector with all its promises can no longer meet the nation's retirement needs. It would take too much money out of the pockets of each and every American worker to get the job done. For its part the PBGC has been a fine idea and has done a remarkable job, but it could be eliminated completely in just a few years if a new independent retirement system were adopted. That in itself would save billions of dollars of bureaucratic expense and continue the down-sizing of government that we hear so much about these days.

In 1983 when Congress set up the new changes in Social Security, it put in place all the necessary components to get the job done with a new, separate system, even though our representatives didn't realize it at the time. For this we owe them a debt of gratitude.

The time is now upon us. The window of opportunity is here!

"I do not choose to be a common man. It is my right to be uncommon, if I can. I seek opportunity, not security. I do not wish to be a kept citizen, humbled and dulled by having the state look after me. I refuse to barter incentive for a dole. I will not trade freedom for beneficence nor my dignity for a handout. It is my heritage to stand erect, proud and unafraid; to think and act for myself, enjoy the benefit of my creations, and to face the world boldly and say, this I have done. All this is what it means to be an American."

Dean Alfange, 1984

10

Federal Government Retirement Plans

"In the main it will be found that a power over a man's salary is a power over his will."

Alexander Hamilton

Have you done any good reading lately about government pensions? Have you ever wondered why your neighbor down the street, who worked for the Commerce Department, has retired at an early age and seems to be well off? Maybe you've heard about a friend who retired at age fifty-seven from a staff job with Congress and is off on a four-month trip to Europe? How is this possible, you ask yourself, when you've worked all your life and still have to work four more years before you can retire and take Social Security?

And what good will that be? You may work for a company that has no retirement plan so the most you are likely to receive in 1995 and 1996 according to the Social Security Administration, is $1,248 per month from Social Security, plus whatever you choose to take from any savings you have accumulated over the years.

These disparities grow worse with every passing year as more workers reach that long talked of plateau, "the elderly level." One glaring exception are those who have reached this stage as government workers. They find themselves in an enviable position, for through the years Congress has seen to it that government pension plans are second to none. In addition, our legislators have added COLAs, those now famous cost-of-living adjustments that make it possible to double such pensions every fifteen years or so. Former Senator Al Gore, Sr. is a classic example. When he retired his pension was at $40,000 per year (more than $3,000 per month). Today it is over $80,000 per year (more than $6,000 per month). All because of COLAs. What retiree in the private sector is that lucky? But if this weren't enough, government workers have a health care system that is the best in the country, or very near to it, paid in large part by the government, and that continues on after retirement.

The United States Office of Personnel Management, which administers all federal pension plans, says that federal pensions are roughly at a level of 25 percent of 1994 payroll. This will climb to 40 percent by the year 2020.

Let's review our government's pension system.

In 1920 the federal government enacted the first retirement plan for its civilian employees. The plan covered over three hundred thousand people at that time and provided benefits for those who retired after fifteen years of service. I note here that there are now twenty or so federal retirement plans serving our vast and complex system of agencies and departments. They all merit discussion but in this chapter we will mention only three.

By 1986 there were 2.2 million federal workers covered by the Civil Service Retirement System (CSRS). The CSRS pension covered all federal workers, including members of Congress, until 1984. Employees could contribute up to 7 percent of their salary, congressmen and judges up to 8 percent, with the government kicking in an equal amount (very much like a current 401K plan). Under CSRS, regular benefits are based on the average of a worker's three highest salaried years. Those employees with thirty years of service are eligible for an annuity of about 53 percent of their highest three-years' salary average.

A revised system called the Federal Employees Retirement System (FERS) was enacted for all those hired after January 1, 1984. The reason for this is that Congress was looking for new sources of income for Social Security so it decided to include all government workers. How did lawmakers sweeten the deal for FERS employees to make shifting to Social Security attractive? The FERS employees can retire at age sixty-two with a three-part retirement plan. First, they will receive approximately 33 percent of their highest three years' salary from the FERS defined benefit pension plan. Second, they will receive Social Security, and they will receive their share of the proceeds from the Thrift Savings Plan as the third part of this retirement plan. (I will explain the Thrift Savings Plan shortly.)

Those employees in the older CSRS were given the option of converting to FERS. As related by one recent federal retiree, most didn't for three reasons. First, the Office of Personnel Management didn't take a very active roll in explaining all the options, and the materials distributed to explain the transfer seemed to underestimate the value of the thrift plan. It was unclear whether those who remained under civil service still were able to invest in FERS, and it was hard to tell if the government matched these investments. The final issue is more relevant to the discussion: those who converted to FERS lost key benefits of early retirement. Employees could retire early at age fifty-five but would not receive COLAs until age sixty-two. During the intervening seven years the base civil service annuity would erode to about half depending, of course, on inflation.

While Congress didn't realize it at the time, and probably still doesn't, this Thrift Savings Plan (TSP) will be the forerunner of a new age in retirement systems. This plan allows government employees to contribute up to 10 percent of their annual salary while the government matches up to 5 percent. With forty years of government service employees could wind up with approximately $1,373,320 in their retirement accounts.

To illustrate how nice this retirement will be just look at the example given in the FERS manual. For a woman or man who retires under FERS in 2016 after thirty years of service as a manager with a high-3 average pay of $47,420, the benefits would be as follows:

Basic FERS (1.1% x $47,420 x 30 years) = $15,650
Social Security   = <u> 7,700</u>
                               Total $23,350

There are now internal offsets that reduce a worker's pension when both Social Security and civil service (or military retirement) benefits are due the same worker. The details were made so complex that the average retiree just throws up his or her hands in disbelief and lets the computer do it.

Such a retirement in itself would be envied by over 70 percent of the elderly in America today. As it stands this annual income would exceed our Social Security retiree's annual amount by several thousand dollars. But that's not all. There is still the Thrift Savings Plan account that this person has invested in for all of his or her years of service. After thirty years this balance will be close to $490,880. Had this person worked five more years this TSP would increase to $824,000 and would go over a million dollars if she completed forty years as outlined in the 1994 TSP brochure. As an added bonus the individual could leave this thrift plan intact until the time benefits are actually drawn. Ultimately this account balance must be transferred upon retirement to an Individual Retirement Account (IRA) or other eligible retirement plan, which means the balance would continue to grow and earn interest.

After age fifty-nine and a half employees may withdraw from the TSP account. In just thirty years of service and investment this would give them an additional $32,725 per year, calculated on a fifteen-year pay out, on this TSP account alone. The pay out period for this C Fund (one of TSP's funds) is strictly up to each individual. Under this scenario that's a grand total of $56,075 per year, when added to the other two parts of this retirement plan outlined previously. And to put the icing on the cake, parts one and two (Basic FERS and Social Security), will grow every year thanks to the congressionally mandated COLAs. Now that's what anyone would call a very nice retirement.

Here is a very interesting comparison to make. Under Social Security the maximum any recipient will receive in 1995 and 1996, according to Social Security Administration, is $1,248 per month or $14,976 per year. In most cases the average working person in the private sector has worked as long and as hard as those in government, has paid the 6.2 percent in Social Security taxes all through the years and winds up with very little to show for it. Is it any wonder that average workers can't understand why something better isn't available to them?

Then there is the perk that takes this pension system out of the "great" column and puts it in the "just wonderful" category. It's a classic work of art by Congress. It's what makes government employees retire with a warm smile on their faces. It's everyone's dream. It's called a COLA, the cost-of-living adjustment a retiree receives each year. All government employees receive it, as well as those on Social Security. It is based on the annual increase of the Consumer Price Index (CPI). This is now done automatically each year as Congress has enacted it into law. This is the bottomless pit that our lawmakers dug for themselves and the thing that almost guarantees budget increases every year. As of 1994, COLAs account for more than half of the $36 billion in annual pension benefits paid to retired federal workers.

Hastings Keith, now seventy-eight and a retired Republican congressman from Massachusetts helped found the National Committee on Public Employee Pensions in 1982 to push for COLA reform. He liked to point to his own civil service pension as a way to illustrate the awesome power of COLA compounding. When he retired at age fifty-eight in 1973 after fourteen years in Congress, he received $18,720 in annual federal pension benefits. Since then COLAs have increased this single federal pension to a total of $71,928 in 1994, according to an article in the October 1990 issue of *Readers Digest*.

This particular example finally opened the eyes of Congress and these gigantic increases have been reined in. A gold star for Congress!

On average a retirement package will double in fifteen years. In what job or position in the private sector can such a pension plan be found? The premise was great, but in trying to help the elderly even more, Congress created a monster called the COLAs, which is now out of control and will be very hard to rein in.

★   ★   ★

Looking deeper into this Thrift Savings Plan, there are three funds to choose from. The G Fund, valued at over $17.44 billion as of September 30, 1994, is invested in short-term nonmarketable U.S. Treasury securities. These are the same type of bonds that are in the Social Security Trust Funds. This means that this fund increases the debt because it will have to be repaid through the normal budget process.

The C Fund is a common stock Index Investment Fund and is invested in a Standard & Poor's 500 (S&P500) stock index fund. The stock holdings held by the S&P500 index fund represent ownership shares in major companies in the private sector, such as General Motors, Wal-Mart, General Electric, and many others. The value of these shares moves with the market and shows in the current price of this mutual-like fund. There is no assurance for future rates of return. That's how it should be, but look how this fund has done over the past decade. This S&P500 index fund for the years 1980 through 1989 has shown an average annual rate of return of 17.46 percent. This C Fund was valued at $5.83 billion as of September 30, 1994, and is the real sleeper of these three funds. Investing in this fund could easily bring over $2 million to an individual's retirement account after forty years of investing.

The third fund, called the F Fund, is a fixed-income investment fund that is invested in a Shearson Lehman Brothers Aggregate (SLBA) bond index fund. By law, the F Fund must be invested in fixed-income securities. It represents a good cross section of the bond market, and includes U.S. government and mortgage-backed securities. Adding mortgage-backed securities to the F Fund, such as Ginnie Maes or Fannie Maes, provides investors greater diversification in the fund. In the past ten years, 1980-1989, SBBIG (Solomon Brothers Fund) and SLHA (Shearson Lehman Hutton Fund) have shown an annual rate of return of 12.38 percent. In fact, in 1992 the overall rate of return was 13.83 percent. As of November 30, 1994, the F Fund was valued at $1.59 billion.

These three funds—G, C, and F—are passively managed for this Thrift Savings Plan. Indexing is a common form of passive management and is used because it is difficult to beat the average return of the market.

Vesting in the Thrift Savings Plan is very simple and conveys to an employee the right to share in a pension fund after a specific period of time. Employees can start investing in the second year of government employment and they are vested after three years of service. Vesting is done in what TSP calls open season. In 1994 this was from May 15 to July 31 and November 15 to January 31, 1995.

In its May 1994 newsletter the Thrift Investment Board showed in very dramatic fashion just how well a government employee could do by investing in the C Fund. The article was called "The Miracle of Compounding" and starts off with, "When you put your money in the TSP, you experience the miracle of compounding." Three examples show how good this C Fund can be.

First, if an employee earning $33,000 a year contributes for ten years from age twenty-five and then stops, his or her balance at age sixty-five will be $1,185,000 (assuming a 10 percent average rate of return). In the second scenario if this employee contributes for thirty years but doesn't start until age thirty-five he or she will have $737,000 (again assuming a 10 percent average rate of return). The difference is the time the money is accruing earnings. In the third case, if this same employee contributes 5 percent of his or her pay for forty years along with the matching funds added by the government, the employee account balance would be $1,747,000 (assuming the same 10 percent average rate of return). The person will have earned over $1,615,000 in compound interest! The chart below illustrates this. These illustrations come from the May 1994, *Highlights* newsletter of the Federal Retirement Thrift Investment Board.

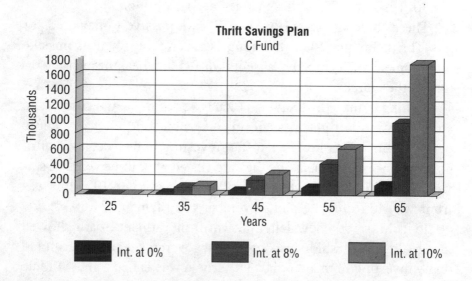

As of September 30, 1994, the three TSP accounts were valued at $24.86 billion, a four billion dollar increase in one year.

These three funds of the Thrift Savings Plan are all great plans and do a very good job in securing the retirement of federal employees. Each government employee has the option of joining any one of these three plans. The G Fund however, has one serious problem that will strain the annual budget because this fund is completely unfunded. Like Social Security, it keeps government Treasury bonds that will have to be paid back it with money appropriated at the time of maturity. This means that each year's budget has a weight on it, dragging it down before it even starts. It's great to have a good retirement program, but what will be the cost in the years to come as more and more employees retire?

The military has not been forgotten in the scheme of things. Those in the armed services do just as well. Since 1957 all members of the military have been covered by the Social Security program, in addition to their own pension programs.

Current estimates put government pension liabilities, according to a December 20, 1992 *Houston Chronicle* story, over $1.5 trillion! Now that is very serious money by today's standards, and this underfunding will continue to increase each year under the current systems. In fact, this retirement liability is now the size of the entire 1993 annual budget. Barely two years ago this pension liability was put at $1 trillion by former Congressman J. J. Pickle. To continue on this path will one day overload the entire system it was created to protect. And to further exacerbate the problem and make it even harder to solve under present conditions, the Social Security System is speeding headlong down this same thorny path, with its $400 billion deficit in tow. Remember, the Social Security deficit will grow to over $1 trillion after the turn of the century.

Let us not forget the designers of these grand systems, namely, our esteemed congresspersons. Our senators and representatives are on the top rung of the pension ladder. One stalwart and dedicated group in Washington, the National Taxpayers Union Foundation, recently conducted a study on pension benefits for congresspersons who would be retiring as of December 31, 1994. Listed below are a number of examples of how much these lawmakers will receive.

Congressman Tom Foley	$123,804 per year
Congressman Bob Michel	110,538
Congressman William Ford	105,787
Congressman J. J. Pickle	96,462
Congressman Dan Rostenkowski	96,462
Congressman Jack Brooks	96,462
Congressman Don Edwards	96,462
Congressman Neal Smith	$ 96,462

These congresspersons, architects of this grandiose plan, will go home telling everyone what a great job they did during their tenure and leave it to others to try and close the Pandora's Box they opened many years ago. All these lawmakers will receive that self-voted, deluxe treatment called a COLA. In approximately fifteen years former congressperson Tom Foley will be in the $200,000 per year range and will see it continue to grow every year for the rest of his life. Now that's going out a real winner. And at whose expense?

Will the newly elected Republicans who are now in the majority have the courage to do what needs to be done or will they just try to gloss over it, as their Democratic predecessors have done? Only time will tell, and that is unfortunate because if they wait too long everyone will pay a much higher price.

The National Taxpayers Union Foundation has also recommended that Congress eliminate the defined benefit portion of the congressional pension system. This is part one (33 percent of their high three years' salary average) and part two (Social Security) of the FERS retirement plan. It further recommended that the only remaining congressional pension should be participation in the Thrift

Savings Plan, which should then be open to all members of Congress. But what incentive does Congress have to change its own retirement programs?

Of course Congress is not the only culprit. This munificent pension system has long been set up for government employees, and defended by the federal employee unions and the administration no matter what the cost. The irony here is that all sides are looking in the wrong direction and have the wrong perspective on the problem. Without a doubt all federal employees under these systems have earned and deserve their retirement. The solution is not to try and cut costs or benefits, or to raise taxes. The right idea is to change the current system to a new concept that will do an even better job without the problems of underfunded liabilities and increased regressive taxes to prop it up. The current retirement system for government employees, as well as the Social Security System, have almost reached the end of their tenure and can no longer be validated. We could, of course, retain those systems for another decade or two, but then they would buckle under the weight of the claims being made on them, thereby facing unpleasant changes.

Solutions to this type of problem are politically driven, as is the case with all things inside Washington. The politicians do not seem to realize that ultimately they stand to gain from this paradox: backing away from the special-interest groups to establish a sound retirement system for all, based on income and growth, similar to the successful Thrift Savings Plan, will bring about what they really want and desire, namely, continued political survival and respect in their districts.

At the same time average workers, whether in government or the private sector, will have a plan they know will be there when retirement time rolls around. And it will be a plan that doesn't depend on regressive taxes. Best of all, it will not be politically motivated or accountable to some government bureaucracy.

No one wants to give up hard-earned gains, especially the elderly. Our elders know that the long road they have traveled is nearing its end. How could they survive if their incomes were cut? It's a sad game our political leaders are playing when they know full well that to continue on in the same way will lead to some very serious consequences within the next twenty years. Fear of change should not stop us. Scare tactics aimed at trying to frighten current retirees won't work. Remember, any new plan will not effect or change the old federal retirement system under which many have retired. Those will simply be phased out.

There is an open secret, which everyone knows, yet few are willing to admit. No one wants to retire. At a certain point in life people may want to slow down, do things a little differently, but never simply retire. They want an income that will give them a chance to enjoy the rest of their lives, and for this they are willing to fight.

Everything that is needed is now in place to reinvent both the federal retirement programs and Social Security, thereby merging them into a new retirement system. This new program will give every working man and woman, whether in government or the private sector, a retirement program similar to the C Fund of the Thrift Savings Plan. It will be safe, sound, and secure, without the horrendous trillion-dollar underfunding on the federal side and Trust Funds gutted of nearly a half trillion dollars on the Social Security side.

Why replace an excellent federal retirement program? The system is great, for the few it covers, but it, too, is a tax base system. No one can fault the federal employees for getting the best deal they can for their pensions. They worked hard and long for many years and have earned their entitlements. Again, it should be made clear that no new retirement plan would undermine or jeopardize what federal workers now enjoy.

Current federal retirees and those over age forty will never be effected by any new system. Only new employees or those who wish to change will be effected, and then only after an act of Congress. The intention is not to replace these federal retirement programs but simply to reinvent them and transform them into a twenty-first-century system based on investment and growth, and not on regressive taxes shouldered by all workers. It has been documented that half of the annual payout from the current federal retirement is the result of cost of living adjustments and this colossal blunder will continue to increase every year under present conditions. If these trillion-dollar underfunded liabilities continue to mushroom unabated they will become an ever-growing burden on each annual budget, which means even more will be heaped on the already overburdened shoulders of American taxpayers.

The new system I will outline in part 3 eliminates this escalating problem and still gives every worker the same, if not a better retirement picture. Under this new scenario a federal worker will have the option of moving into and out of the federal or private sectors at anytime without any loss in retirement benefits. The same would hold true for those in the private sector.

It is time for the working people of this country to stand up and insist on a sound, fiscal retirement. Remember, there are over half a million people (many of whom are voters) to every one member of Congress! In a test of wills is there any doubt about who would win?

"Arouse his will to believe in himself, give him a great goal to believe in, and he will create the means to reach it."

John F. Kennedy, 1960

11

State Retirement Systems

"In a democratic world, as in a democratic nation, power must be linked to responsibility and be aligned to defend and justify itself within the framework of the general good."

Franklin D. Roosevelt, 1945

State pension plans are simply fifty smaller versions of the federal government's retirement systems for its employees. Each state has the same problems on a smaller scale, because state officials have practiced and copied what the Washington officials have done. Both have one thing in common, they feed from the public trough.

Statisticians tell us these days that approximately 40 percent of our income goes toward paying taxes of one sort or another. It just goes on and on. A penny here for the city, a penny there for the county, several more for the state and everyone cringes when Washington starts playing their tax-saving games. We usually wind up paying more. It's no wonder that hardly anyone can put aside enough to retire on. It's a wonder that there is anything left in the public trough after these political entities take what they claim to need.

How is it that everyone who works for the state for twenty-five years, from public officials to teachers, is deserving of a pension, while the rest of the state's population is not? There is no doubt that teachers who have worked that long have well earned it and deserve the pensions they receive. Teachers have their own retirement systems in the various states whose legislators opted them out of Social Security. For instance, in Texas this was done in 1937. Since then the Teachers Retirement System has provided pension and other benefits, such as death and disability benefits, for all Texas teachers. It is a very sound system and today provides benefits for 129,000 retirees and covers approximately 600,000 active members.

But this current retirement system for the state of Texas does not mean that retiring teachers will be living in the lap of luxury in retirement. For instance, in Texas the 1994 Teachers Retirement booklet shows that after twenty-four years of creditable service an average teacher will receive $1,368.16 per month from the retirement plan. Based on a life expectancy of approximately twenty-one years after retirement, a member could expect to receive $354,627 or more for contributions of $26,051.41. The legislature may very likely grant further increases in the future.

Those teachers who reach the top of the pay scale and have worked for forty years with a three-year high average salary of $38,000, will receive $2,533 per month upon retirement. The plan also includes the normal disability and survivor benefits. In 1995 the contribution rates were 6.1% for the member and 7.31% for the state. Teachers in Texas do have several nice options to their retirement plan. First, if they leave prior to retirement they can take the accumulated balance that they have put into the fund plus accrued interest with them when they leave. The state contribution only comes into play when the teacher actually retires. Can workers who leave their jobs in the private sector take their Social Security contributions (that's the FICA withheld from their paychecks) with them in a lump sum? We all know the answer to that! Wouldn't that be a great idea. Second, they have an early age retirement clause. They may retire at age fifty-five with thirty years or more of service with full benefits, or they may retire at any age with thirty or more years of service but at a reduced standard benefit until they reach age fifty-four. In fact they can retire at age fifty-five with only five years of service also at a reduced standard annuity.

There seems to be a double standard in effect here, one for organized groups like teachers, and one for the rest of us. There are millions of workers in the private sector who work for small businesses and put forth as great an effort to see their jobs are done well, and yet they have no pension or retirement plan toward which to look forward.

What is the difference between those workers who are paid with public money and those in the private sector? The one difference is that state legislators have decided to take care of those on state payrolls and they have the authority to pass laws and levy taxes. But taxes should be used for the entire public good, not just for the good of a few.

As we have seen, teachers are in a separate category from other state workers, and their unions have constantly knocked on the door of the state legislators seeking increased wages and benefits over the years. In most cases they have earned these increases, and understandably we all try for the best wage we can get, but what about the nurse who works for a small hospital or the lady who works for a small air conditioning company that cannot afford a retirement plan? Don't these hard-working women deserve the same comprehensive retirement? The only difference between these women and the teachers is that the teachers' bosses control the public purse.

Many states these days have gone into the lottery business to increase their revenues, ostensibly to increase funds for schooling, which of course will include teacher pensions. Who does the woman at the air conditioning company go to? After she has worked forty years and has paid all her taxes, what does she have coming for a retirement? According to the 1994 Congressional Research Report, the average benefits for a retired worker is $674 per month from Social Security. The system has been so mishandled by Congress and the administration over the years that even that retirement benefit is in question.

Let's look at it another way. As of July 1994 there were 18,378,000 citizens (and who knows how many illegal aliens) in the state of Texas. There are twenty-seven congresspeople and two senators. There are now 729,000 active and retired teachers, and as of February 1995, there were 250,534 employees on the state payrolls. That leaves 17,398,466 citizens of Texas to think about. Of course a number of these Texans work for the federal government, the military, and for cities and counties throughout the state and so are covered by other and various pension plans. The tax dollar is being spread pretty thin these days. Then of course, a number of Texans work in large industries that have retirement plans of one sort or another.

This leaves over 13 million or some 70 percent of the citizens of Texas out on their own, to take care of themselves, and yet at the same time their taxes help to pay the cost for all these other Texans who are covered by various government retirement plans. Isn't it time to "level the playing field" for all the working people in Texas and in every state throughout the country? Let's give all 18 million Texans an even better chance at a secure retirement based on their efforts and not one subject to the whims and notions of state and federal legislatures.

Using taxes to pay for retirement programs is fast becoming as archaic as the model T Ford. Its days are passing. Various government entities are already proving this to be the case. It has been done quietly and without any fanfare for nearly two decades in a number of city and county governments. It is only a matter of time before the pendulum swings completely to investment and growth as the means to get the job done for everyone.

For all the assets and investments in the various state pension funds they still are underfunded by $50 to $100 billion, an amount that will continue to grow as the years go by unless something is done. These billions are the taxes that each and every one of us will have to pay in the future. Our various state legislatures have committed us to them. To continue on this road when there is a much better superhighway waiting to be used is questionable at best. Is it any wonder that a new idea is needed!

All fifty states have picked up the federal government's habit of underfunding. Some are a great deal worse than others. By 1994 only three states were fully funding their pensions. State legislators have also realized that expecting the public to bail out poor fiscal management has its repercussions. California learned that lesson some years ago when the property taxes got so high that Howard Jarvis started a ballot initiative called Proposition 13 to freeze taxes at current levels and we all know what happened there. It passed by a resounding margin.

Underfunding of pensions on the state level simply means that the amount owed to the pension funds will have to be provided in the future rather than now. This is where statistics and actuaries come in: based on sophisticated computer models and past experience, the state guesses at what it will need for the future retirement of all the state employees. When legislatures make these projections they are in effect telling us what taxes are going to be needed for years to come. It's not much different from you or me deciding to buy a car or home on time payments. We make the commitment—say we'll pay—and if we want to keep that car or home we have to make the payments each month. The only difference is that we must get our money from income, while the state acquires its money through taxes and fees. In choosing to fund pensions in this way, legislators start tying their own hands. They take on a heavy liability. If there is a downturn in the economy and the revenue projections are far too optimistic, the state could face a real crisis.

Thus far, the federal and state governments have committed up to 40 percent of everyone's income for the foreseeable future in order to fulfill promises legislators have made in the name of their constituents. For those citizens who never thought they had a reason to vote, they do now. Your money is being laid on the line whether you like it or not. You should know where your legislators stand on pension funding.

In order for the average taxpayer to really feel this liability, each of us should be required to write out a check (or checks) each pay period for these taxes rather than have them deducted. When these taxes are simply being deducted from payroll, employees begin to feel that the net pay *is* what they are getting. The taxes that the state and federal governments receive automatically become hidden liabilities that only the employer sees or feels. The self-employed are the workers in our economy who see what is happening because they literally do pay all their taxes themselves and can see just how much of their income is committed to public use.

All these retirement plans in the fifty states take on added burdens as they grow. Each state from time to time goes through a cash flow crisis. In these periods they begin to look at state pension funds for cost savings and even at times have tried to raid them. One city wanted to borrow money from the employees pension fund to give a pay raise to the very employees the fund covered!

In 1987 the Wisconsin legislature, according to the annual report of pension funds, took $84 million out of the public pension fund of the Wisconsin Retired Teachers Association to pay a benefit previously funded by state taxes. Neither working nor retired teachers were consulted and as a result pensions were reduced. The state of course was sued and the teachers won. However, appeals are still in process.

For the most part all fifty state plans are run by honest, hard working, and dedicated individuals who do their best to see that the plans grow and prosper to secure the retirement of the state employees.

Today there are over $3 trillion in assets in all these various state pension funds. It's becoming big business and many brokerage houses are trying to influence pension fund trustees to allow them to manage their funds. Many funds buy the bonds of their state and political subdivisions to help the state or local economy and to earn good interest rates.

Hiring outside financial advisors has been a popular practice of fund managers to make such crucial decisions, but many such decisions have been based on friendships or political relationships rather than on competitive assessment of financial skills. Regrettably, this has been the ugly result of people who cannot resist temptation. As the funds grow larger this type of risk is bound to grow. Having in place a strong independent auditing system is a vital deterrent to such mismanagement.

An even better deterrent would be to offer public disclosure of the fund's activity on an annual basis. After all, the state's citizens are footing the bill; state employees are simply the recipients. While employees should know what is going on with the pensions, it is the taxpayers whose money makes it all possible. Such disclosure is even more vital today because these systems are becoming so huge. Taxpayers should know what is in the future of these funds and what their state legislators have permanently added to the state's annual expenditures, and in so doing increased the tax burden of all income earners in the state.

In California in 1994 the Calpers Fund had over $79 billion in assets. These fund managers had been talking about investing in corporations with the idea of having control. The idea ostensibly was to push for greater profits and in doing so receive larger dividends for the state pension funds. The idea of political entities having control over private sector companies is as foreign to the thinking of this country as it would be to have a king.

Returning to our key concern about underfunded state plans, the following list is offered for your consideration.

STATE & YEAR	INVESTMENTS OR ASSETS (IN BILLIONS)	UNDERFUNDED AMOUNTS (IN BILLIONS)
California (1992)	$59.0	$7.2
Colorado (1991)	11.2	1.0
Illinois (1992)	3.4	2.3
Maryland (1992)	12.7	5.9
Maine (1991)	1.9	1.3
Michigan (1993)	5.4	1.1
Florida (1993)	5.8	1.6
New Jersey (1992)	30.8	2.4
Ohio (1990)	20.6	5.5
Wisconsin (1990)	16.1	1.9
New York (1992)	41.2	7.5
South Carolina (1992)	13.9	2.2
Tennessee (1991)	$ 9.4	$1.6

The information shown here is taken from each state's annual report for the year indicated. Underfunding is a very simple term. It means that the taxpayers owe the state workers and teachers that much for their retirement in the future whether they like it or not.

Today, on average, state governments spend 14.3 percent of payroll costs on pensions; local governments, such as cities and counties, spend about 17.5 percent. The federal government spends about 25 percent of its payroll on retirement benefits. Compare any of these figures with private companies that keep their pension costs to 3.6 percent of their payrolls and you begin to wonder what is going on.

Two of the major rivers in southern Russia, the Syr Darya and the Amu Darya that have their headwaters in the mountains of the region near the Afghanistan border, flow north into the Aral Sea. The Aral once measured over 26,000 square miles, was 235 miles in length and 180 miles wide. Years ago the Russians began to use these once mighty rivers for the irrigation of the cotton farms in the provinces of Uzbekistan and Turkmenistan east of the Caspian Sea. When these two provinces became republics of Russia in 1925 the Aral was the fourth largest inland body of water in the world. Irrigation was the answer to progress and subsequently cotton became a major export from this region.

The idea seemed to be good at the time but, because of overuse, by 1975 these once great rivers had become mere trickles compared to what they had once been. In turn the Aral's water receded dramatically and its salt content rose. This exposed salt on the dry seabed sounded the death blow to all plant life. The area is now turning into a desert wasteland, and changing the climate around the sea. The cotton farms now need more fertilizers, pesticides and most of all, more irrigation. It is estimated that the Aral Sea is now down to half its original size and its final destruction is less than thirty years away.

Like the use of the waters flowing into the Aral Sea, pension funding for state employees is an ever growing fact of life. The money rivers keep flowing into these funds and yet the source of those funds, they should really be called taxes, is beginning to dry up. What is down the road is anyone's guess, but we all know the source is not endless. And the problem remains: the demands for benefits are growing even larger, just as the cotton farms of the Aral basin demanded more and more irrigation. The taxpayers of each and every state should know what liabilities their state representatives have placed on their shoulders for the future.

The states choose to opt out of Social Security in favor of their own pension plans so they can get better financial results and have tighter control. As the pension funds grow larger the state politicos look at all these funds and wonder how can they divert some of the money to reduce the pressures on the state's budget. Since the system is dependent on politicians for increased funding and growth of benefits, the fund managers must work with the legislatures to achieve the goals of the fund.

But the states and counties are beginning to feel the same squeeze that Washington has felt for many decades. The funding problem cannot be solved any longer by the usual taxing and spending methods. These lawmakers, too, are running out of new sources of revenue. Regardless of what kind of tax is initiated or fees for services affixed, it still comes out of one source, the taxpayer's pocket. The content of that pocket is getting leaner. Government entities have bitten too deeply into the source. Quite possibly this is why state lotteries have become such a big hit. These revenue sources are not taxes and still they bring in huge amounts of money.

An interesting situation has arisen over the past decade that adversely affects state employees. Having their own retirement systems meant they weren't touched by the rules governing Social Security. But, as usual, Congress discovered a way to deny some of these retirees their due. For example, if a teacher had another job in addition to teaching, that person would have to pay Social Security tax on the outside income, but when it was time to retire, Social Security could and would reduce the teacher's benefits by as much as two-thirds because he or she would be receiving a teacher's retirement. Where is the fairness here?

Many U.S. congressmen and senators as well as interested groups cling to the old thinking that Social Security is an icon that can never be touched. They say that means-testing (in other words, an examination into the financial state of a person to determine eligibility) is wrong and should never be considered, because it hurts the system as well as the recipients it supports. Yet that is exactly what Social Security is doing to retired teachers' benefits if the retiree has other retirement income. What else is it but means testing when the government taxes 85 percent of your Social Security benefits if you earn outside income above a certain dollar amount?

There is a better way to handle retirement, but first the government has to realize that it can no longer handle the programs it currently administers. It is just too big for them, and getting bigger all the time. It looks like Congress is fresh out of new ideas. It can no longer get a handle on the problems, because its members are trying to appease everyone. That just can't be done. It shows that politicians and bureaucrats cannot solve the problems. Dedicated statesmen could. It is time for a new system, a system that is completely independent of Congress and the administration, a system that is sound and operated by the people it serves, an independent system that has been tried and successfully field-tested for nearly two decades and found to be a winner.

It is time for the Social Security Independent Banking Corporation (SSIBC), featuring the Individual Security Retirement Account (ISRA). The third part of this book tells the whole story of these two innovative concepts. The proposal is presented in layman's terms so that everyone can read and understand it. It is time to privatize!

12

Where Do We Go from Here?

"The aspirations of most of our people can best be fulfilled through their own enterprise and initiative, without Government interference."

Dwight D. Eisenhower, 1955

Social Security and retirement plans, whether they are private or among the many government plans, can stir our emotions more than most any subject we can name. Why? Because they hit home like nothing else does. Many of us have seen our parents, grandparents, friends, and neighbors go through some pretty trying times, when it comes to those so-called golden years of life, and we don't want these experiences to be our final reward for all the decades of hard work and struggle we have endured.

Since the days of FDR, Congress and the president have given us a dream called Social Security, and all Americans have grabbed

167

onto the idea that this was our retirement and that it was secure. Why did Americans believe in such ideas? Because they trusted Washington to get the job done. For decades we have been told that Social Security will always be there and that it will help us when it's our turn to retire. Playing on our passions, legislators and presidents throughout the middle and late twentieth century have established programs which they knew would have good short-term results, but long-term effects that could be devastating.

Social Security worked well for the first four decades and then things began to change. The short-sighted thinking of Congress inspired constant increases in benefits to retirees without providing the tax base necessary to support them. Then lawmakers topped it off by creating cost-of-living adjustments (COLAs), the cost of which could bankrupt the system. Second, the population explosion after World War II stretched the current overburdened system to the breaking point with large numbers of people soon to make claims against Social Security for benefits.

It's entirely possible that the newly elected Republican-controlled Congress will make changes, but the system is well beyond any band-aid approach. It needs major surgery. In fact the best approach would be to lay the current system to rest and start a completely new program. Congress makes all sorts of promises and yet does nothing even when it knows that Social Security is broke.

What has happened to the federal pension plans is almost as unbelievable. Building retirement systems on regressive taxes and the fluctuating moods of legislators is no way to establish a long-lasting and sound federal retirement system. In fiscal 1996 the federal retirement program will cost $64.4 billion and the costs grow every year.

Private systems are not far behind in needing to divest themselves of the defined benefit plans that hold the employer responsible for the entire plan. In addition, more government regulations and the realization of the company's fiduciary responsibility, regardless of the annual profit picture, could point a bleak future for corporate

America. If these plans are to survive they must be turned into defined-contribution plans or 401Ks.

With very few exceptions, how many of us have stopped to realize that all the retirement plans in this country are built on an adversarial relationship. This applies to most pension plans in the private sector as well as those in the government, both state and federal. It especially applies to Social Security. In the early days companies such as the American Express Company set up retirement plans as a way to thank employees who did their best to help the company during their working years. Social Security was set up, as we all know, to give a small measure of relief during the lean years of the Great Depression. Government pensions were established for similar reasons, but also because it was a way to garner votes.

But through the decades vast changes have been made. New forces were added to the equation. Unions were formed in both the private sector and government agencies because the workers found it very hard to stand up to the employer, to bargain for better working conditions and wages. Together these workers were a force with which to be reckoned. How true that was. The unions became a powerful force in the battle for greater benefits. From that day forward the relationship between the employer and the workers became adversarial.

The U.S. Congress has used Social Security as a tool to gain re-election, either by offering more benefits or claiming that political opponents would try to deny benefits to retirees. And we are all well aware of what federal lawmakers have done to Social Security through the last several decades with very little regard for its recipients. The battle that was joined a generation ago gives neither side a peaceful way to end the conflict in the present form, and it remains that way today.

A change must be made. In order to have a successful retirement program this adversarial factor has to be eliminated. Retirement is an individual matter tailored to the specific needs of each person. The golden age of retirement does not have to disappear if we have the courage and foresight to shift to a sound and sensible approach, one that recognizes the limits of the current system. We must learn from our past mistakes and move on to better methods.

In a March 30, 1995 letter to this author, Senator Alan K. Simpson (R-Wy.), Chairman of the Social Security Subcommittee, had this to say.

> Do know that I still have deeply serious concerns about the long-term solvency of Social Security and I will continue to be very honest about those concerns. It would be much easier to just say that "everything will be okay." After all, I won't be the one here in the Senate who has to deal with these problems in the year 2014 or 2029. However, changes will either come in the form of thoughtful planned change, or in the form of bankruptcy and reneging on our pledged obligations. We will then have doomed our descendants to permanent poverty if we hide from these facts and simply choose to "do nothing." Fortunately for us, we have the opportunity to act on our own behalf as well as theirs.

Part 3 relates a whole new story. It is a concept that is fair to both the old and the young alike. It eliminates the battle between generations, and also the adversarial relationship, because the money used to invest in this new concept belongs to and comes from the individual and will always remain that way. No longer will the private sector or the government have to worry about allocating funds toward retirement plans. It sets up a system that takes care of current recipients and those ready to retire, while at the same time establishing a new system for the younger generation that is based on investment and growth, not on regressive taxes. In fact, it takes taxes completely out of the picture as a basis for retirement.

It closes down the Ponzi scheme problem since the system will be sustained by only current investment. The federal government will no longer have to worry about how it is are going to repay over $500 billion that Congress appropriated from the Social Security Trust Funds since that money will never be needed for future retirement. How many other plans have you read or heard about that gave a half trillion dollars back to the federal government?

Then to add a very nice touch, this concept will return to the private sector over $170 billion a year once the system is fully phased in. Imagine how much good private business could do for the economy with the infusion of this much capital. And since this would not be borrowed capital the effect would be that much greater.

PART THREE

The Revolution That Must Come

13

The Solution Begins:
The Window of Opportunity Is Here!

Lexington and Concord came into sudden glory on April 19, 1775, when the minutemen engaged a sizable force of British army regulars in the first battle of what would become the Revolutionary War fifteen months later, in July 1776.

There on the North Bridge at Concord was where the first shot was fired that the nineteenth-century American poet Ralph Waldo Emerson said "was heard round the world." It was fired by minutemen who were really just angry farmers and townspeople. Their anger stemmed from the fact that the king and government in London were not interested in listening to the average people in the Americas. The Americans were there at Concord because they knew the time had come to stand up and make some changes for the good of the colonies—and so it must be with Social Security. It's time for everyone to stand up and demand a real change.

For hundreds of years the majority of people seldom lived to reach the age of sixty-five. But the twentieth century changed all that. With the advent of modern medicine, better food preservation, improved sanitation methods, and other advances people began living longer. It was something that Congress didn't realize until it was too late.

During the sixty years since the Great Depression of the 1930s average working men and women have come to think of Social Security as their retirement in the future. The government encouraged this thinking and so workers gladly paid their FICA because they trusted that the government would take care of them when they reached sixty-five. Little did anyone realize what the government actuaries already knew, that few people in the thirties were expected to live past the age of sixty-five. With all that has happened over the years one would wonder about the planning that was done in these early administrations.

As we have said time and time again, Social Security's basic idea is a very good one, but the more its structure is looked at, the bleaker its future becomes. Twenty more years down this current road of siphoning off every nickel from the trusts funds could spell untold economic disaster for millions.

Recall our discussion of what is called a Ponzi scheme. In this inverted-pyramid scheme, those few who enter (invent) first receive ample financial rewards, which sparks increasing numbers of people to think they, too, will reap large benefits. But as the program grows and takes in greater numbers of recipients the money generated is spread thinner and thinner until there is not enough left to cover everyone. The program depends on an ever-growing influx of money, which is an unlikely prospect. In the Social Security system, the ratio of workers to retirees is falling all the time. Decades ago it was 16.5 workers to 1 recipient, and today it is down to 3.2 to 1. If it were to get close to one to one, what would be the point of this Social Security system at all?

Both of these retirement ideas, Social Security and private or public retirement plans, will simply collapse on themselves unless some very real changes are made during this small window of opportunity that has come to us and will be available for the next several years prior to the next major influx of retirees. This window of opportunity is simply a period of time during which no one will be penalized. If we wait too long things will get expensive one way or another.

The senior citizens only want a fair shake and if they see a plan that is better for all concerned they will back it all the way. That is what the ISRA plan is. It's a sound program for all generations.

The time is fast approaching when the government will be talking about trillions of dollars, not just billions of dollars to take care of Social Security. This will happen within the next two decades, according to knowledgeable people, including a former commissioner of Social Security. Continuing under the current program would mean that Congress would have to bite the bullet and decide whether to raise taxes or lower benefits. That is why a new Social Security plan is now needed for retirement. The current system is dangerously close to being out of control.

The Individual Security Retirement Account (ISRA) program is offered with this time frame in mind. It answers the current needs of the elderly and those retired; keeps the Baby Boomers, who now number some eighty million, in the program so they also will receive and earn a sound retirement program; and sets the younger generations up in a new system that will give them a retirement plan that is second to none, one that will not depend on the whims of Congress and the administration, but on sound investment principles.

All this will be laid out in layman's language in the next four chapters. All the legalese has been removed so that anyone can read and understand it. Unfortunately, this is not true of the Social Security information we receive today. It's virtually impossible to understand without the help of a lawyer and an accountant. How did we ever stray so far away from a common language?

Then there's the outrageous idea of taxing Social Security benefits. If you have saved and invested for years, the government now is penalizing you for having a head on your shoulders and the good sense to take care of yourself.

The Democratic administration of 1993 talked its Democratic colleagues in Congress into upping the rates and taxing you even more on Social Security benefits if your income is over a specific figure. How did members of Congress who have said they are against means testing let this get by?

In the proposed Individual Security Retirement Account (ISRA) system there will be no taxes on retirement income. Of course, this will have to be written into law. There are more than enough ways to raise taxes without resorting to taxing retirement benefits. In fact, when Social Security is taken out of government's hands the budget and the deficit will be seen in a completely different light. Without the Social Security Trust Funds to bring huge revenues into the Treasury, the debates over budgets and the deficit will be more realistic. The national debt will not be artificially reduced by the billions that Social Security brings in each year. We will have a much truer picture of what we owe as a nation.

Then this system, once in place, will give Congress a very easy way to completely eliminate the billions of dollars worth of IOUs that the Treasury owes to the current Social Security Trust Funds. More on this in later chapters.

Second, this ISRA concept will set a specific rate for all workers, i.e., the 6.2 percent now being withheld, and it will never change without the approval of the workers themselves. How's that for a real change! This is outlined in detail in chapter 20. It will all happen because the new concept will take the Social Security system out of the hands of Congress and the administration and set up an independent system that will be responsible to only one group of people, the working men and women of America.

In a real twist, one that will have Congress talking to itself and the administration wide-eyed, the business portion of the FICA tax, the matching 6.2 percent, will no longer be paid by business. This will actually be phased out, as will be outlined and discussed in chapter 18. To give this much, over $169 billion annually, back to the private sector may cause heart palpitations to many in government, and business, too, but can you think of a better way to improve the economy and create thousands of new jobs? The give-back will not be in cash but rather a tax abatement. This is one of the many good side effects of the new program.

As an example, in 1993, Mr. Robert Crandall, head of American Airlines, held a conference in a large auditorium in Fort Worth, Texas, which many personnel of American Airlines attended. He pointed out that American Airlines had lost over $500 million in the past year and said it could not continue this way. Mr. Crandall outlined three problems: salaries, wages, and benefits.

Just think of how these three problems could be turned around very easily, and at no expense to anyone, if American Airlines did not have to pay into the Social Security system the 6.2 percent on wages up to the current maximum. In addition, it would no longer have to worry about any retirement plans for its employees. Why? Because neither would be necessary under the new ISRA concept. The chapters to follow will show how.

American Airlines is in the flying business and should not have to be in the retirement business. This holds true for every business, large or small. In the early days it was no problem. A few people could handle the retirement end of the business. But no longer. In addition to huge staffs, the funds have to be accrued, deposited, and invested. Then there are all the rules and regulations of the federal and state government, as well as any and all agreements with the various unions. It has become a big job.

Let us give some mention to the various welfare programs that are attached to Social Security as barnacles on a ship. We are all for giving a helping hand, but few realize how far Congress has taken us down this path. Today there are some seventy-six programs that fall under the heading of welfare. If you would like to explore this morass ask your member of Congress to get you a Congressional Research Report on the subject.*

A number of these programs are administered by the Social Security Administration but are funded by general appropriations and not Social Security taxes. Let's start with the federal Supplemental Security Income (SSI) program, which was enacted by Congress in 1972 and went into effect in January 1974. The unified program ended the multiplicity of other assistance programs formerly administered at the state and local levels. Under the SSI program eligibility requirements were made uniform. SSI provides monthly cash payments to any aged, blind, or disabled person whose income is less than a stipulated amount ($4,080 per year, as of January 1, 1987). To qualify as an aged person, an individual must be at least sixty-five years old. Federal SSI payments and the administrative costs of federally administered state supplements are financed from the federal government's general revenues.

In addition, there are other programs such as SSI Benefits for Children with Disabilities, Food Stamps, and Aid for Families with Dependent Children (AFDC). These are worthy programs and should be continued and administered as they are now, with appropriate safeguards built in to curb abuse.

There are other benefits under the Social Security system now that should and will be included under the proposed new ISRA program.

First there is the extension of benefits to dependents and survivors that was legislated into law in 1939. Then there is the death benefit that is payable to the survivors of workers who die from work injury. Both of these programs will be discussed in chapter 18 to show how they will be handled in the new ISRA program.

One other program should be touched on here. Today Medicare stands on its own, as 1.45 percent is deducted from everyone's paycheck to provide the necessary funds. This program has been linked

---

*"Cash and Noncash Benefits for Persons with Limited Income," #93-832EPW.

to Social Security only by the fact that it is administered by the Health Care Financing Administration (HCFA), under the overall responsibility of the Secretary of Health and Human Services, and is mentioned only to show it is a completely separate function and has really nothing to do with retirement. This deduction is now shown on each individual's paycheck as a separate item. Congress is at this time in 1995 trying to move funds around with Social Security so that Medicare will not go broke. In addition, the Republican-controlled Congress this year is setting a new agenda to prevent Medicare from going broke. This agenda will save over a trillion dollars in seven years by simply slowing the rate of growth.

To emphasize the need to update and bring the Social Security system into the next century it's enough to read the many newspapers throughout the country. As an example, an article titled "Workers Expect Social Security to Short Change Them, Study Shows" was published by the Fort Lauderdale *Sun-Sentinel* early in 1993 and later picked up by the Houston *Chronicle*.

Written by Ellen Forman, it began with a note of deep concern:

When it comes to Social Security, many of today's workers are getting a little nervous. Unlike today's retirees, whose benefits far exceed their contributions younger workers see themselves putting in more than they'll ever get out.

Many say they would like the option of putting part of their Social Security taxes in other retirement plans, such as Individual Retirement Accounts. But pulling out of the trust fund could be dangerous to the economic health of Baby Boomers when retirement comes, experts say. It is also agreed that without Social Security many workers wouldn't save at all.

It is not surprising then, to find younger people have less faith in Social Security. Some 65 percent of eighteen to thirty-four-year-olds of those surveyed said they expect to pay more than they will get, compared with half of those fifty-five and over. Also 50 percent of eighteen to thirty-four year olds think Social Security should be voluntary, compared with 40 percent of those fifty-five and over.

A blue ribbon panel dubbed the Committee for Economic Development (CED), comprising 250 of this country's top business executives and university presidents stated in a recently published report dated March 1995 that "America's retirement system is underfunded, over regulated, and soon to be challenged by unprecedented growth in the retirement-age population. Consequently, our nation will confront a major crisis in financing the needs of the elderly at the beginning of the twenty-first century."

This thought-provoking account, detailing one of the greatest financial challenges facing us in the coming decade, was the result of the direct efforts of the CED Subcommittee on Pensions and Savings, chaired by Lawrence A. Weinbach, Managing Partner and Chief Executive of Arthur Andersen & Co. The CED is a nonprofit, nonpartisan, and nonpolitical independent research and policy organization dedicated to the betterment of humankind. Its report went on to say, "If action is postponed, the nation will face the very unpleasant choice of a substantial cut in the economic status of the elderly or an economically damaging and unfair tax burden on future generations of workers." This enlightening report is appropriately titled, *Who Will Pay for Your Retirement? The Looming Crisis.* Now there's a title that's straight to the point!

The report goes on to cite the problems immediately ahead of us. First there is the anticipated sharp decline in the ratio of workers to retirees. To compound the problem, private savings are at a woefully inadequate level and, as we have discussed, underfunded pension promises abound in both public and private plans. Then finally the rapid growth in government spending for the elderly threatens to get so far out of control that when the baby-boom generation retires, the claims on the Social Security system could not be financed by reasonable burdens on taxpayers. The report concludes, "But it is now

clear that the Social Security system has made promises to future retirees that cannot be kept without vastly improving prefunding or im-
posing a harsh burden on future workers."

The question that begs an answer is this: "If 250 of the country's
top executives and university presidents can see these horrific problems and over 90 percent of the citizenry concurs, then why does
Congress hesitate to make the necessary changes? In 1994's November election, when America's voters said forty years of
unchecked entitlement growth was enough, they emphasized the
point by deposing the sitting Speaker of the House who refused to
listen to his constituents. The stage was then set for many sensible
ideas for retirement to emerge.

The Committee for Economic Development has shown a great
deal of foresight and judgment in clearly outlining the problems of
Social Security and pension plans that are almost upon us. To solve
these problems in a lasting fashion, halfway measures will never do.
An entirely new outlook and concept is needed. Simply to continue
doing the same old thing—increasing taxes and reducing benefits—
is enough to make everyone shake their collective heads in disbelief.
These old solutions just lead to the same old results.

In an October 1995 executive summary for the Third Millennium, a younger generation group from twenty-five to thirty-five,
Richard Thau reported, "The United States is moving inexorably toward reforming its national retirement system. The recent prolifera-
tion of grassroots organizations and coalitions indicates that public
opinion is shifting to a new way of thinking about Social Security.
Within this context, young adults, the generation that will foot the
bill for the Baby Boom's retirement, must understand the Herculean
burdens they are expected to shoulder over the coming decades. Not
surprisingly, members of this Generation X are remarkably pes-
simistic about the long-term viability of Social Security. At the same
time, they are woefully ignorant about the possibilities for reform."

Such articles and many others like them show clearly that most people in this country realize that changes must come to make Social Security fair for all working people. A March 1995 Houston *Chronicle* article shows that a poll found overwhelming support for the ultimate answer to the Social Security conundrum. Young Americans want the freedom to invest all or part of their Social Security payments in private retirement accounts. A staggering 82 percent want this freedom.

The Katy Independent School District, in a suburb of Houston, Texas, has tackled a youth problem in a sound and sensible manner. They set up the Katy Youth Sports Association so that all the young school children of their district would have a chance to play in the various sports programs, such as basketball, soccer, and baseball without regard to their talent. Everyone is given a chance and encouraged to achieve greater things than they thought were possible. Children and young adults are not thinking about Social Security or retirement. And this is how it should be. These issues lie well beyond their immediate concern. It will be up to the current generation to set things straight for their futures and those who come after.

Every generation has its own unique set of challenges, but to saddle future generations with the trillion-dollar deficits that are sure to come in the current Social Security program is unthinkable. Is this the kind of heritage we wish to leave to our children? We who are old enough have seen unbelievable changes since the Great Depression of the thirties.

We now have a once in a lifetime opportunity to take a beleaguered retirement system and develop it into a unique plan that will benefit future generations without creating liabilities that could turn a promising life into a nightmare of debt. We have to make the effort, both for ourselves and for our grandchildren.

14

The Beginning of New Ideas

"If there is a lesson for us, it is that we, as a free people, must be prepared for change so that when it comes, we're ready to meet new challenges and opportunities. Our system of government is unique and best able to change and to move forward without disruption or break in continuity of purpose."

Ronald Reagan, 1982

A new factor quietly entering into the retirement equation makes this idea timely as well as viable—the economy has become mobile! No longer do workers enter the job market with the idea of remaining with a company for their entire working lives. Companies now merge, are bought out, or fall by the wayside as new products or mega-giants change the business climate. This led to fewer workers being eligible for company pensions. But under this new concept, with the employee's money invested in an independent retirement system, the problem is eliminated and the equation changes dramatically in favor of the worker

Now with the prospect of a new retirement system, the working men and women of this country, who have had a great many doubts about Social Security in the past several decades, can take back their system and know the freedom to enjoy the golden years of their lives, without the constant wrangling of bureaucrats.

On the surface at least, in recent years, Congress seemed to be making limited progress toward Social Security reform. It pointed with pride that the Social Security Administration had been given the status of an independent agency. Independent from what? The only thing Congress did was fire the secretary of health and human services, one of the bosses. Everything else remained the same. Even President Clinton's new 1995 budget shows the full use of the Social Security Trust Funds surplus to mask the true deficit. Congress and the administration, over the years, have reached a point at which they only act when a crisis looms overhead. Crisis management does not usually include any long-range planning. To be completely fair, there are those in Congress who realize that the Social Security situation is almost to the point of complete collapse and are still trying to do something. Consider this case in point. On January 5, 1993, Congressman John Porter (R-Ill.), reintroduced his bill H.R. 306 in the 103rd Congress. Congressman Porter had introduced this bill in the previous Congress but Democratic chairmen blocked its progress through key committees. In his bill Congressman Porter would cut Social Security taxes by two percent and refund the money to the American workers in the form of an Individual Social Security Retirement Account (ISSRA). This account would be in the worker's name but could not be touched until retirement. This accumulated amount could then be deducted from the Social Security benefits each person would receive upon reaching retirement age.

"This two percent tax cut," Porter explained in an April 15, 1991, news release from his office, "not spent but saved, will build and grow with compound, tax-free interest throughout their working lifetimes." He said investment safeguards would be established. He also said that denying the federal government the Trust Fund reserves by placing them in ISSRAs "would discipline the system and ultimately help bring down interest rates and stimulate economic growth."

The congressman further wrote in the Chicago *Tribune* on April 6, 1991, "Workers retirement funds would be protected from congressional profligacy and would be there when needed. The Social Security system, an immensely successful program that has largely eliminated senior poverty in America, would continue to meet its obligations. Every American worker would become an investor in our economy and have a direct stake in its success."*

Congressman Andy Jacobs (D-Ind.), Chairman of the Subcommittee on Social Security, finally held a hearing on H.R. 306 on October 4, 1994. The scope of the hearing was to present testimony to analyze types of alternative investment for Social Security. The Congressional Budget Office (CBO) report presented examined investing trust fund assets in the private sector and the estimated results. This hearing also looked at the idea of establishing individual retirement savings accounts and the impact of its implementation. Congressman Jim Bunning (R-Ky.) made the following statement at the hearing: "In my mind the central question is on balance, weighing all the advantages and disadvantages, is the Social Security System in concept unchanged for almost sixty years now the best way to assist Americans of all economic levels to provide financial security for themselves and their families?" The congressman hit the nail right on the head, and the American people know the answer.

There were twenty-nine witnesses after CBO Director Robert D. Reischauer testified. Many were in favor of keeping the present ar-

---

*For further information see: General Accounting Office report, December 1990, "Social Security, Analysis of a Proposal to Privatize Trust Funds."

chaic system. Taking exception were a number of witnesses who actually did listen to the people, analyze what has been going on for years and discuss new ways of getting better results for the elders of coming generations.

The progressive, up-to-date thinking of Carolyn L. Weaver, Ph.D., Director of Social Security and Pension Studies for the American Enterprise Institute, during her testimony at this hearing, illustrates very succinctly the increasingly popular viewpoint. In part, Dr. Weaver said, "I wholeheartedly support proposals to shift toward private investment of social security monies—provided that the government is kept at bay and not left in a position to play the market or to influence others to do so."

Two options would move in this direction. The first, modeled after the supplemental retirement system for federal civil service employees, known as the Thrift Savings Plan, would involve subcontracting the investment of trust fund monies to competing professional money managers who would be authorized to invest in particular mutual funds (see chapter 11 for further details).

Compared to the present management of Social Security, this option is attractive because it removes surplus Social Security receipts from the federal coffers and thus improves the chances that Social Security will not contribute to a loosening of fiscal control in the rest of the budget. In addition, by introducing a mixed portfolio of bonds and equities (stocks), while leaving open the allocation of monies to various funds, this option affords the opportunity to take at least partial advantage of known or anticipated trade-offs between risk and return which might result in a higher average return (or more favorable risk-adjusted return) on trust fund assets. Compared to direct private investment by the government, this option is attractive because it depoliticizes investment decisions to a significant degree.

Two problems would remain, however. First, the Congress could still use its powers to influence the allocation of capital and thus the distribution of wealth and income in the economy. The Thrift Savings Plan largely escapes this problem by virtue of the fact that individuals participate on an entirely voluntary basis.

Second, this option, like direct private investment by the government, fails to deal with a central problem under present law, which is that nothing prevents monies raised today through the payroll tax from being spent later—by Congress, not by money managers—to increase Social Security benefits or to pay for part of the cost by selling assets. The Thrift Savings Plan avoids this problem by virtue of the fact that it is a defined contribution plan. Under such a plan, contributions (and interest earnings) are fully vested; monies invested belong to participants and cannot (absent fraud) be diverted for other uses.

A more promising approach is to move further in the direction of the Thrift Savings Plan, giving individual workers (not a government board or private money manager) the right to control the investment of some or all of their Social Security taxes, as Congressman Porter had in mind.

Dr. Weaver concluded that "The inefficiencies of the present system derive in no small measure from the government's monopoly control over trust fund investments, coupled with its inherent monopoly over fiscal policy. In view of this, expanding the powers or discretion of the federal government to manage trust fund investments would be most unwise."

At the same October 4th hearing on Social Security, William G. Shipman, principal of State Street Global Advisors, Boston, Massachusetts, testified. Having spent more than twenty years in institutional financial research and consulting, he put it very concisely in his statement: "Given the dependence of retirees on their Social Security benefits, the precarious financial condition of the system, and young workers' abysmally low return on their FICA tax, it is incumbent upon society to craft a lasting solution. Another tax increase and benefits cut is not the answer. In my view, the solution is a transition from a government run pay-as-you-go program to a private system of retirement accounts. The transition must unequivocally ensure that the elderly are not hurt, for they are the least able to adjust. It also must capitalize on the fact that equity and fixed income returns are infinitely superior to those of a pay-as-you-go system. The transition also should be as short as prudent investment practices will allow. Lastly, economic incentives should be encouraged."

Congressman John Porter's idea to create an Individual Social Security Retirement Account (ISSRA) for each worker is a very good one, but it has one problem that is difficult to overcome. The life expectancy is now estimated at approximately twenty years beyond retirement age, according to a Government Accounting Office (GAO) report and the Social Security Trustees Report of 1994. Even if Porter's plan were adopted immediately the estimated outlay of revenue for retirement claims would exceed the income generated by the year 2015, some say sooner. Nevertheless, Porter's bill was a good first step and it was headed in the right direction. It would take congressional hands out of the trust funds: rather than investing in the growing national debt, the funds would be invested in the future of the workers of this country, where they rightfully belong.

This was certainly not the first Social Security reform proposal offered. Back in 1986 conservative congressman Newt Gingrich (R-Ga.), now Speaker of the House of Representatives, trotted out another interesting idea. He intended to propose a radical reform of the Social Security system in which the government checks would gradually give way to private retirement accounts for most retirees. The congressman was going to suggest that the payroll tax be replaced by a national sales tax that would finance Social Security benefits for today's older Americans. He further proposed that businesses would be required to pay their 7 percent payroll tax directly to workers under age forty. The workers in turn would be required to set up mandatory Individual Retirement Accounts. The government would be responsible for maintaining all senior citizens above the poverty level.

His proposal undoubtedly was done with "tongue-in-cheek" but had a number of interesting ideas. One in particular would abolish the current income tax on Social Security benefits and repeal all provisions that discourage working after age sixty-five. True to his character Gingrich was not afraid of looking at new ideas.

A number of outstanding writers in the 1980s came up with similar interesting ideas, of which the Houston *Chronicle* featured many. One suggested that the Social Security assets should be invested in real assets instead of the federal debt, so that those assets would earn real money and be available when needed. Other prominent articles were:

July 27, 1982: "Social Security to Borrow $7 Billion"
August 18, 1982: "Social Security Questions Must Be Answered"
November 9, 1982: "Study Calls for Major Social Security Changes"
November 7, 1986: "Radical Social Security Reform Pushed"
November 12, 1989: "Divvy Up the Social Security Surplus and Put It All in IRAs?"
February 12, 1990: "Take Social Security Private"

The J.P. Morgan Company concluded that the only safe approach would be "to privatize just the surplus portion of the Social Security revenues" (that portion over and above what is needed to meet the current obligations of the system) by giving each taxpayer his or her own share of the surplus in the form of an IRA-style account that would be off-limits until retirement, and would be invested entirely in sound securities. This could be used to lower the Social Security payout at the other end by the amount accumulated in the individual IRA account.

The value of this idea has been developed and refined in a paper from the U.S. Chamber of Commerce, which shows that by putting the average worker's share of the Social Security surplus into an IRA account at conservative yields, those retiring in the year 2018 would have in their accounts as much as $58,000 to $75,000. Releasing such liquidity to the marketplace would provide hundreds of billions in new capital to the private economy. One significant virtue of the proposal is that it finally faces up to the fiction of a "building surplus" in Social Security.

All of these ideas are well worth considering, so why is no one in the leadership in Congress considering them? The answer is very simple. Everyone skirts the real issue. Congress can no longer handle Social Security. The system has out-grown congressional review. These distinguished legislators haven't acknowledged it yet, but Social Security as we know it is coming to the end of the road. Letting go of such a huge revenue generator and spending machine will be hard for lawmakers, but let go they must, because Social Security is now a full-blown retirement system.

The American workers are now insisting that this should be their retirement system, and the new Republican Congress, in order to make this so, will have some very hard choices to make. But for the rest of the working people of America it will be a great day, because their futures will no longer be dictated by Congress when it comes to retirement.

As we have seen, a growing number of people in this country agree, at least in principal, with the need to reform Social Security. In fact, many people on Main Street America no longer feel that Social Security will take care of them in retirement, and they place the blame squarely on Congress, which seems to have no thought of the future of the American worker.

Of course, there are the rare exceptions. Congressman Porter's idea was on the whole well received by economists, magazine editors, and publishers. Several well-known columnists and a few independent groups said many positive things about his proposed ISSRAs. Indeed, the effort to privatize retirement plans has gained international attention with plans being implemented in France, Great Britain, Switzerland, Japan and especially Chile. The years after World War II were hard for all of these nations, but after their economies were revitalized through such programs as the Marshall Plan, they worked out plans for the retirement of their senior citizens. Its time we took a good look at their results and think about how their plans could help our own Social Security system.

Look at Chile, a country that has been proving this over the past several decades. Its economy has been growing over ten percent per year for many years now, because its people have been investing in themselves. This growth is not, to any great extent, from the use of outside capital. Chile has been able to maintain a steady economic growth rate and at the same time develop over the past several decades a Social Security system that takes care of its elderly in a fashion much like the ISRA program to which I have alluded.

Many of these new ideas are good ones and are definitely focused in the right direction, but not to the extent needed to overcome the problems Social Security faces. Economists worry about the tremendous amounts of money that a new system, independent of the government, would have at its disposal for investment purposes, but that really doesn't hold up in light of today's ever-growing economy. In 1945, who ever thought there would be over two trillion dollars invested in the stock market and mutual funds in 1995, and a similar amount in bonds of various types? In twenty-five years, assuming normal growth, this figure will more than triple. Our economy can absorb these funds and more as new and different industries are established and grow.

True, there will have to be safeguards written into this new plan so that the new Individual Security Retirement Account (ISRA) program would not, and could not control any firm, business, or industry by owning controlling stock interest. (These restrictions are discussed in later chapters.) This would allow and encourage individual wealth as each person's ISRA would become part of the person's estate to be passed on to designated heirs, while at the same time keeping it under control by taxing wealth that is passed on in the form of inheritances. This in effect will give both state and federal governments a new source of income, and the cycle will continue.

In 1912 Woodrow Wilson said, "America lives in the hearts of every man everywhere who wishes to find a region where he will be free to work out his destiny as he chooses." What greater right do we have than to determine our own destiny, and that of our families; to provide not only a retirement for ourselves, but to leave family members the funds to prosper and grow? As Theodore Roosevelt said nearly a hundred years ago, "No country can long endure if its foundations are not laid deep in the material prosperity which grows from thrift, from business energy and enterprise."

It is hoped that this ISRA program, when it is fully explained, will show people what can happen when a small amount is put away each pay period. It can accumulate into a savings (in addition to the ISRA) that will give workers peace of mind in the future.

Some might wonder why it has been proposed that a 6.2 percent payroll deduction for the employee to be deposited into his or her ISRA. Why not take current 3.1 percent collected from the individual and 3.1 percent in matching funds from the employer? There are several very good reasons not to go this route. The primary reason is that the 3.1 percent from the employer will be needed for more than a decade to help fund the retirement of present Social Security recipients (chapter 19 explains further). Second, after everyone is on the new system, this percentage will translate into much more than its current value of $84 billion dollars. Giving this large sum back to the business community is by far the best way to create new jobs and by extension a large revenue base for government.

New product testing has always been a sound idea and a guiding axiom in industries where new products are the key to success.

Working out the anomalies before the product goes into production for market consumption saves time and money, as well as the company's reputation. While this is particularly true in pharmaceutical companies, the airline industry, and computer software manufacturing, to name but a few, the area of retirement is not all that different. Before outlining this new concept for the Individual Security Retirement Account program let's see how the idea has been working in south Texas where such a plan has been in place for almost two decades. This narrative points out the ironic twist to the current rhetoric that is coming out of Washington, and we can only hope that its full meaning will not be lost on those in Congress.

In south Texas, along the windswept Gulf Coast, where multitudes of hurricanes have made their landfall over the centuries, the three counties of Galveston, Brazoria, and Matagorda are proving that there are better ways to handle a retirement program for the hardworking folks of this land, rather than depending on the federal government to do everything. Until the early eighties government entities, such as cities and counties, had the right to opt out of Social Security and establish their own retirement system. This option had been provided when the Social Security Act was passed in the thirties.

In 1979, then County Attorney Bill Decker came to Don Kebodeaux, a highly successful businessman, and asked him if he could devise a plan so that Galveston County employees could opt out of Social Security. Don pondered the problem and called in his friend, Rick Gornto, a leading financial expert, who was later to become his partner. These two businessmen, realizing the coming problems in Social Security, designed a new program for political subdivisions that would provide a retirement for employees that was many times greater than the standard Social Security program of the federal government. These two entrepreneurs proved to be decades ahead of everyone in their financial thinking and planning. In the late seventies these two Texas entrepreneurs organized a company that was later to become the First Financial Capital Corporation of Houston, along with its operations affiliate, First Financial Benefits Corporation, to operate and administer such plans.

The men from First Financial Capital took their ideas to Galveston County and presented them to former County Judge Ray Holbrook and the Commissioners Court in 1980. When Judge Holbrook and County Attorney Decker saw the wisdom and foresight of this concept they took charge and shepherded the plan through its various stages.

Debates were held throughout the county between Social Security representatives and the men from First Financial for the benefit of the county employees and to answer all their questions. Balloting on the question was held in 1981. By a resounding vote of 78 percent to 22 percent, the Galveston County employees endorsed the idea and the county opted out of Social Security.

The local unions fought the idea at first, and several Galveston County officials also opposed the action. But as time went on and they learned more about the program nearly all of them saw the sound judgment in this course of action. Years later retired County Attorney Bill Decker was to tell the story of how a number of union ladies working for the county thanked him for his wisdom and guidance. They said at first they had serious doubts about giving up the fixed income of Social Security, but now that they were getting ready to retire they were very happy they did. They were much better off for having made their decision.

"The Alternate Plan has been a godsend for Galveston County and clearly improved employee benefits" said Judge Holbrook recently in a March 23, 1995, letter to me. "The 22 percent who voted against it in 1980 are all supportive now and see the many benefits of having a retirement program other than Social Security, which most employees under age forty believe will not be there when they retire. And now no one objects to the mandatory feature which was made part of the plan a few years after it started. For governmental employers who can mandate participation in a retirement program, The

Alternate Plan was the way to go. It was a real blow against freedom and free enterprise when Congress outlawed the opt-out feature." Judge Holbrook, who retired in 1994 after twenty-eight years of distinguished service, concluded by saying, "Of all the things I accomplished while county judge, setting up this retirement system for the Galveston County employees is one of my proudest achievements."

The plan implemented in Galveston County was very simple. The 6.13 percent rate that had been taken out of workers' pay for Social Security now went into the pension fund for employees and was matched by the county. In recent years the county increased its participation to 7.65 percent which included premiums for the life and disability insurance. Life insurance and disability insurance were included at first to match exactly the Social Security benefits. Later they were improved.

Tolbert Newman, the point man for First Financial Capital and First Financial Benefits, the operating arm, who handles the overall responsibility for these plans for the three counties, sites the following example of the growth that can be achieved in this pension fund, now called The Alternate Plan. If an individual is twenty-five years old and makes a $2,000 annual contribution for ten years, assuming an 8 percent earnings rate, this individual will have $314,870 when he or she retires at age sixty-five. If the person continues on for forty years, the pension will be over a million dollars, and *that* is for each and every county employee.

In addition to the Alternate Plan retirement package, The plan's disability and survivor benefits are provided to eligible employees at no cost. The premium cost of this coverage is paid by the county, as part of its 7.65 percent matching funds. The life insurance benefit for those under age seventy is 300 percent of the worker's annual earnings with a minimum benefit of $50,000 and a maximum of $150,000. Social Security doesn't even come close.

Seeing this tremendous potential, in 1982 Brazoria County, Texas, followed suit and opted out of Social Security in favor of The

Alternate Plan. A year later Matagorda County came aboard. Both of these counties went in at 6.7 percent, increasing a great retirement plan to a higher plateau.

The idea was taking hold in a big way. The entrepreneurial spirit was alive and well. In a short period of time the idea spread and some two hundred other counties, as well as many cities, in Texas, and throughout the entire country, saw the latent possibilities of the program and were ready to become candidates to opt out and join the plan that First Financial Capital Corporation had devised and was now administering. Don Kebodeaux, the moving force behind this venture, and his partner, Rick Gornto, the plan designer and architect, clearly demonstrated that if left alone enterprising Americans can set up retirement systems second to none. It also proved that the government itself was the biggest part of the problem.

Then as these other political subdivisions in Texas and throughout the country began to set the wheels in motion for this farsighted change, up jumped the devil. Social Security had gone broke the year before and Congress was looking for ways to bail out the system. Capitol Hill had already decided to hit on the federal employees and then got a rude shock when it looked like all employees of the various counties in Texas, and elsewhere, were about to opt out of Social Security. That was a calamity Congress couldn't allow at this critical point, so it canceled the opt out clause in 1983. Fortunately Galveston, Brazoria, and Matagorda counties had their systems up and running so they were permitted to continue.

The Alternate Plan that began as a fledgling up-start employee benefit plan has stood the test of time and proven that it can and does outperform Social Security. The plan that started in Galveston County ended the first year with a modest balance. Today, with over five thousand employees from these three counties, the Alternate Plan has grown to a very healthy and sizable portfolio. Not only did the investment portfolio grow tremendously but as a result of the tireless efforts of First Financial many costs in the programs have gone down significantly. The alliance between the employees of these three counties and First Financial Capital and its operations affiliate, First Financial Benefits, proved to be a real winner. The working people of this country would do well to look at the results of the efforts of Don Kebodeaux, Rick Gornto and First Financial Capital Corporation.

If we go back to chapter 11 and compare the Galveston plan to the Thrift Savings Plan, we wouldn't find a great deal of difference. In both cases every employee upon retiring at age sixty-five will have over a one million dollar fund set aside to meet their retirement needs. (Note: The total dollar amount for each employee for retirement will vary and will be based on the employee of either plan completing the necessary requirements of each plan, such as length of continuous service and amounts invested.)

The real differences can be found when the Galveston plan is placed alongside today's Social Security. The Galveston plan is built on a solid foundation of investment and growth through the use of compound interest over time rather than being propped up by withholding taxes. The plan cannot be changed without approval of the employees; it is not at the mercy of the whims and moods of Congress. The Galveston Plan does not have unfunded mandates and it is not stabilized by a tax-based budgetary process. The plan is supported by the people it serves, not by the nation's taxpayers.

Surprising isn't it that the largest elder group in America, AARP, keeps telling seniors that Social Security is the only way, and $1,248 per month is the best they should expect, when $5,000 to $9,000 per month can be just as easily obtained through sound investment? True, for those now in retirement, $1,248 per month, plus the cost of living adjustments (COLAs), is all they can expect, as a maximum, but it is a different story for those in their prime working years.

No one is planning to, or will ever, abandon the current recipients or those who will be retiring under the current system. They should continue to receive the same Social Security benefits they do today, including COLAs. The new program will only affect future generations. That is the unique feature of the new Social Security Investment Banking Corporation (SSIBC), a system designed for both young and old, to be fair to both, without penalizing anyone.

The next four chapters tell the story of how all working Americans can benefit in the same way as the folks in Galveston, Brazoria, and Matagorda counties.

15

The Individual Security
Retirement Account

THE FUNDING

The Social Security system was started with a simple payroll withholding approach, called the Social Security tax. It has worked well through the years, but the time has come to change this tax into an investment vehicle for the working people of America. How can it be done and why change now? A simple story will illustrate the need for change.

Two friends, Mark and Jim, graduated from college with their degrees in business administration. Both intended to set up their own retirement plans since they knew that the Social Security System would never cover their needs when they retired, no matter what rhetoric happened to be coming out of Washington. Mark went to work for a large electronics company, where he received several promotions. He did not marry until later in life and throughout his career he put away $2,000 a year in an IRA. In ten years he had started a nice retirement fund. Jim secured a nice position with an oil company. He married a year later and had two children. At the end of ten years he had not even started on his retirement plan. Instead he found himself with a huge mortgage, payments for two cars, and the expense of two growing children. Just how far can a paycheck go? Jim is the mirror image of the millions of working people in this country. It is well known that only four in a hundred people are able to start a retirement plan, and therein lies the need. It takes a very dedicated person to sacrifice the need of today for the future some forty years down the road. When you're twenty-five retirement seems an eternity away.

The great news is that the funding of the Individual Security Retirement Account (ISRA) is there right now for each and every worker. It's the Social Security tax (FICA) taken out of each individual's earnings each pay period. From this withholding money, which now will be an income-producing vehicle, the ISRA program will be funded. It is for this very reason that the FICA withholding must remain in effect and its continuation legislated into law when the program takes effect. The Social Security Investment Banking Corporation (SSIBC) will be set up as a quasi-governmental entity, but will be run as a private enterprise system.

While this new system will look similar to a defined contribution plan, individuals will not have to decide how much to invest in their plan or where to invest it. All contributions (that is the FICA deductions) will be funneled to the SSIBC, where these funds will be handled much like a very large mutual fund. The basic financing will remain as it is now under Social Security: 6.2 percent will be withheld from the employee's wages by the employer each pay period.

To illustrate the accumulated growth of the funds we will use an example of a $38,000 income in the base year as the starting point. This amount will be indexed (increased) by 5.1 percent per year, since this is the average annual projected increase used by the Social Security Administration in 1994, as detailed in the 1994 Trustees Report.

Each employee will also have the option of increasing this amount each year, or at the start of a new job. Employees will advise their employers in writing regarding the amount they wish to have withheld in the coming year. Only at the beginning of each year can this be done, but the amount withheld can never be lower than the base amount, as indexed, i.e. 6.2 percent of $38,000 (the example used in this case), plus a 5.1 percent increase for each succeeding year. Example: the plan can withhold 6.7 percent of $38,000 for the second year.

All these funds withheld from the employees will be deposited monthly to their regular depository (i.e., banks), as is done now by all employers. The employer will recap quarterly as is done now on Form 941. All these 941 forms will be sent to the Social Security Investment Banking Corporation (SSIBC). This will give the SSIBC the information it needs to credit each individual account, and the monies to be received in the normal banking process. Much more will be said about the investment banks in later chapters.

The bank branch where each account resides will remain the depository regardless of the number of jobs each individual has during his or her working days, or where the jobs are located. Proof will be furnished annually by the SSIBC as to the deposits and interest accrued, as well as withdrawals. An annual financial statement of the SSIBC will also be furnished to each individual, giving full disclosure of all investments, assets, and liabilities.

There is also the question of past contributions made to the current system. For those remaining in the current system this does not apply. For those changing to the new ISRA system no credit or vesting will apply, no benefits will ever be paid because of any past contributions to the old system. The current system is a pay-as-you-go plan, so the FICA payments contributed today go toward paying current retirees and do not build anything for the future.

Those retirees coming under the new ISRA system will not need their Social Security contributions since the future contributions and growth of their invested money will greatly overshadow anything they would receive under the current system. For example, young people in their twenties would have almost two million dollars in their ISRA accounts when they retire, giving them over $9,000 per month as a retirement benefit. Can Social Security do this?

Then, too, there is the personal satisfaction of knowing that your Social Security contributions have helped many of the elderly now in retirement. Keep in mind that those elders may very well be your parents and grandparents.

It is also possible that Congress might allow those who enter the ISRA system to deduct the amounts paid to Social Security over a period of time as a contribution deduction on their income tax return. Regardless of what the government calls it this FICA tax remains an income tax under as assumed name.

The ISRA is the individual retirement plan for each working man and woman and will be handled by the SSIBC. All FICA funds withheld (this will now be a real withholding since it will no longer be a tax, and should be called by another name such as Individual Annual Withholding) will go into the twelve districts of the SSIBC in a way similar to a very large mutual fund (more on this in chapters 20 and 21). In this way all growth and also the risks will be shared equally.

The following example is used to show the growth of an ISRA account for a worker through the person's normal employment years. Sample figures used are based on norms for 1995.

Based on the withholding of 6.2 percent from each individual paycheck to the maximum income of $38,000 (our example) in the base year, and future annual adjustments, the following table shows the growth of the Individual Security Retirement Account fund over the years. It is assumed the average man and woman will work forty-seven years. The average wage will be indexed and adjusted on an annual basis of 5.1 percent.

Other statistics are as follows:

Base year payment: $2,356
Annual payment increase: 5.1%
Interest: 6.5% per annum
Years worked for compounding: 47
CPI/Inflation rate: 4%

6.5% COMPOUNDED ANNUALLY

YEAR NO.	PAYMENT EACH YEAR	YEAR END BALANCE	ADJUSTED FOR INFLATION	CPI ($)
1	$ 2,356	$ 2,509	$ 2,415	1.04
2	2,476	5,309	5,013	1.08
3	2,602	8,426	7,806	1.12
4	2,735	11,887	10,805	1.17
5	2,875	15,721	14,022	1.22
6	3,021	19,960	17,469	1.27
7	3,175	24,640	21,160	1.32
8	3,337	29,795	25,110	1.37
9	3,507	35,467	29,333	1.42
10	3,686	41,699	33,845	1.48
11	3,874	48,535	38,662	1.54
·12	4,072	56,027	43,803	1.60
13	4,280	64,227	49,284	1.67
14	4,498	73,192	55,127	1.73
15	4,727	82,984	61,350	1.80
16	4,968	93,669	67,977	1.87
17	5,222	105,318	75,028	1.95
18	5,488	118,009	82,529	2.03
19	5,768	131,822	90,505	2.11
20	6,062	146,847	98,981	2.19
21	6,371	163,178	107,986	2.28
22	6,696	180,916	117,550	2.37
23	$ 7,038	$ 200,171	$127,702	2.46

6.5% COMPOUNDED ANNUALLY (CONT.)

YEAR NO.	PAYMENT EACH YEAR	YEAR END BALANCE	ADJUSTED FOR INFLATION	CPI ($)
24	$ 7,397	$ 221,059	$138,476	2.56
25	7,774	243,707	149,906	2.67
26	8,170	268,250	162,029	2.77
27	8,587	294,831	174,881	2.88
28	9,025	323,607	188,504	3.00
29	9,485	354,743	202,939	3.12
30	9,969	388,418	218,231	3.24
31	10,477	424,824	234,426	3.37
32	11,012	464,165	251,574	3.51
33	11,573	506,662	269,726	3.65
34	12,164	552,549	288,937	3.79
35	12,784	602,080	309,264	3.95
36	13,436	655,524	330,767	4.10
37	14,121	713,172	353,511	4.27
38	14,841	775,335	377,561	4.44
39	15,598	842,344	402,988	4.62
40	16,394	914,555	429,867	4.80
41	17,230	992,351	458,274	4.99
42	18,109	1,076,140	488,292	5.19
43	19,032	1,166,358	520,008	5.40
44	20,003	1,263,475	553,511	5.62
45	21,023	1,367,990	588,897	5.84
46	22,095	1,480,441	626,267	6.07
47	$23,222	$1,601,401	$665,726	6.32

In this forty-seven-year span of time you will have paid in $432,360.

A second example illustrates what a better return of 8 percent would give over a working lifetime.

Base year payment: $2,356
Annual payment increase: 5.1%
Interest: 8% per annum
Years worked for compounding: 47
CPI/Inflation rate: 4%

8% COMPOUNDED ANNUALLY

YEAR NO.	PAYMENT EACH YEAR	YEAR END BALANCE	ADJUSTED FOR INFLATION	CPI ($)
1	$ 2,356	$ 2,544	$ 2,450	1.04
2	2,476	5,422	5,123	1.08
3	2,602	8,667	8,035	1.12
4	2,735	12,314	11,201	1.17
5	2,875	16,404	14,639	1.22
6	3,021	20,979	18,366	1.27
7	3,175	26,087	22,403	1.32
8	3,337	31,778	26,770	1.37
9	3,507	38,108	31,489	1.42
10	3,686	45,138	36,582	1.48
11	3,874	52,934	42,075	1.54
12	4,072	61,566	47,993	1.60
13	4,280	71,113	54,363	1.67
14	4,498	81,660	61,216	1.73
15	4,727	93,298	68,581	1.80
16	4,968	106,128	76,491	1.87
17	5,222	120,258	84,981	1.95
18	5,488	135,806	94,088	2.03
19	5,768	152,900	103,850	2.11
20	6,062	171,679	114,309	2.19
21	6,371	192,294	125,507	2.28
22	6,696	214,910	137,492	2.37
23	$ 7,038	$ 239,703	$150,311	2.46

8% COMPOUNDED ANNUALLY (CONT.)

YEAR NO.	PAYMENT EACH YEAR	YEAR END BALANCE	ADJUSTED FOR INFLATION	CPI ($)
24	$ 7,397	$ 266,868	$164,016	2.56
25	7,774	296,613	178,661	2.67
26	8,170	329,166	194,305	2.77
27	8,587	364,773	211,008	2.88
28	9,025	403,702	228,834	3.00
29	9,485	446,243	247,852	3.12
30	9,969	492,709	268,134	3.24
31	10,477	543,441	289,756	3.37
32	11,012	598,809	312,799	3.51
33	11,573	659,213	337,347	3.65
34	12,164	725,087	363,491	3.79
35	12,784	796,901	391,326	3.95
36	13,436	875,164	420,953	4.10
37	14,121	960,428	452,477	4.27
38	14,841	1,053,291	486,011	4.44
39	15,598	1,154,400	521,674	4.62
40	16,394	1,264,458	559,590	4.80
41	17,230	1,384,223	599,893	4.99
42	18,109	1,514,518	642,722	5.19
43	19,032	1,656,234	688,224	5.40
44	20,003	1,810,336	736,556	5.62
45	21,023	1,977,867	787,882	5.84
46	22,095	2,159,959	842,376	6.07
47	$23,222	$2,357,836	$900,222	6.32

This retirement program would also have a very positive effect on lower-income wage earners. Some people would prefer to go on welfare since they believe they would, for a short period of time, receive greater benefits from the state and federal governments. This type of thinking is erroneous and very shortsighted. This may not be true much longer since the Republicans in 1995 have legislated new reductions in many welfare programs. Welfare is a negative and does not contribute to any Social Security vesting you could receive when you reach the age of retirement. It also does not accrue any benefits in the proposed new ISRA program. Only wages you have earned validate this process. It also takes away the work ethic and lulls people into a false sense of security.

For instance, in the restaurant business these days an average busboy would pay $1,054 while a server would pay an average of $1,619 annually in FICA taxes. When these workers reach age sixty-five, under today's Social Security system they would receive approximately $610 to $780 per month to retire on. Not a great amount, but if they had been on welfare they would be entitled to nothing.

Under the proposed new Individual Security Retirement Account program the busboy and server would now have a much more interesting future. When these folks retire under the ISRA program their retirement plan would pay more than they earned during their working years. For example, using an 8 percent return and indexing at 5.1 percent annually, the following would result:

	Monthly payout at age 65*
Busboy	$5,690
Server	7,310

*Based on a ten-year life expectancy after retirement.

Savings is the key to this retirement system. Even an annual savings of only $600 per year will total out at nearly $293,000 at the end of forty-five years. The "thrift ethic," as some have called it, must once again be instilled in the thinking of the average person today. There is nothing wrong with being average. With a little planning anyone today can wind up a great deal better off than their parents when they reach retirement age.

To save only $600 per year need only put away $11.54 per week, (not a very large amount) *but it has to be every week.* That's the key. As the old saying goes "from little acorns mighty oak trees grow." Very few of us start out at the top, but we all can start with the determination to do something for ourselves. Looking to the government for everything is no solution. That type of thinking stifles both desire and imagination.

In all cases the lives of workers in the new ISRA plan would be insured up to $100,000 as outlined later in this chapter. In this case if a busboy died after ten years his heirs would receive $45,138 from his ISRA retirement account and $54,862 from the SSIBC insurance program. This would provide the family with the financial support to pick up their lives and move on.

What better way to get people off welfare than to show them what the future holds if they want to work for it. The key word here is "work." Remember, you have to work to become part of the ISRA system. And what you invest you keep. Unlike Social Security all the money in your ISRA account becomes part of your estate when you die. The actual outcome of the program may be much better than even my figures show. The two rates shown in the previous schedules are on the conservative side when they are compared to many mutual funds, but they more than cover the inflation rates for the past forty years.*

Today, in the United States, the amounts invested in all stocks, including mutual funds, exceed $3.2 trillion dollars with 1995 showing an even greater increase. Similar amounts are invested in various types of bonds. The investment brokers and bankers have done their jobs well and continue to do so. Why then should we leave trillions of dollars in the hands of a small group of politicians who haven't a clue how to make it grow to help those whose elder years will depend on their good judgment? Many members of Congress

---

*The inflation rates for the past forty years from the Department of Labor Statistics are as follows: ten-year rate of 3.8 percent; twenty-year rate of 6.2 percent; forty-year rate of 4.3 percent.

are well intentioned and do an admirable job of representing their constituents. What makes us think that they are experts in the field of investment and fiscal growth as well? Fiscal matters should be left the professionals who are trained in the appropriate fields.

According to an old saying, "It's a wise person who when she or he doesn't know the answer, knows where to go to get it." To prove the point, there are many excellent mutual funds. As an example, the Fidelity Magellan Fund is a group of mutual funds with over $25 billion in assets. Its average growth over the past twenty years is as follows:

1-year rate (1992)	20.10%
3-year rate	15.68%
5-year rate	17.49%
10-year rate	16.68%
20-year rate	22.77%

There are many other excellent mutual funds that show growth patterns over the years that have greatly outperformed inflation. Some of these are: Twentieth Century Ultra at 20.1 percent, Kemper Growth at 19.1 percent, Aim Constellation at 18.4 percent, CGM Mutual at 17.9 percent, and John Hancock Sovereign at 17.2 percent,

These figures are for 1993. In fact there are over 4,000 mutual funds today and most of them have exceeded inflation over the years.

Now, exactly what happens when you actually retire? Individuals will decide when to retire and just how much they want to withdraw each year, with the only limitation being that their annual withdrawals cannot exceed the amount reached by dividing their balance by their projected life expectancy. Thus, if a person's life expectancy is fifteen years beyond retirement age, and his fund balance at retirement is, say, $800,000, then he can withdraw no more than $53,333 during the first year of retirement. Payments will be made monthly or quarterly. And what happens if the individual outlives his expected life span? In the ISRA plan, money will still be in the fund because each year the daily balance continues to draw interest and when interest is accrued on such large sums, there will be more than sufficient funds to last through a person's retirement days and then some.

In addition, upon retirement, each retiree will receive a single, one-time payment of 10 percent of the total retirement fund, up to a maximum of $100,000, in the base year. This will be an optional feature that can be exercised at the individual's discretion. Each succeeding year this one-time initial payment will be increased (indexed) by 5.1 percent.

Assuming that the one-time payment has already been taken and the retiree is drawing his or her maximum benefit payment per year, should a major problem arise, the individual may withdraw no more than five percent in one lump sum figure, but must show proof of such a problem to the Social Security Investment Banking Corporation. If these restrictive provisions were not added, temptation would be on everyone's mind. We all know how easy it is to spend money and the trust fund was set up to last through the whole of our retirement years.

The following table illustrates how ISRA funds will be withdrawn upon retirement. In this example we will use the 8 percent return figures from the previous table. In this case we will start with an account that has accumulated $2,357,836.

First, deduction is made for the one-time payment of $100,000 withdrawn the first month of retirement. Then, if it is found that the retiree has a twenty-year expected life, the person will use the figure of 240 months. This will outline a maximum withdrawal of $9,824.31 per month. The option is the retiree's. Certainly annual withdrawals can be less, but never any more than the maximum. If less than the maximum allowed has been withdrawn, at the beginning of any new year, the retiree may adjust his or her monthly income up or down as desired.

The following sample schedule is based on withdrawing $9,000 per month, and factoring in 4 percent inflation while using the 8 percent interest growth rate.

Year No.	Account at Start of Year	Withdrawal at Start of Year	Monthly Withdrawal	Account at End of Year
1	$2,357,836	$100,000	$ 9,000	$2,256,944
2	2,256,944		9,360	2,223,546
3	2,223,546		9,734	2,184,266
4	2,184,266		10,123	2,138,221
5	2,138,221	75,000*	10,528	2,008,266
6	2,008,266		10,949	1,945,947
7	1,945,947	50,000*	11,387	1,759,303
8	1,759,303		11,843	1,676,699
9	1,676,699		12,317	1,585,158
10	1,585,158		12,809	1,484,127
11	1,484,127		13,322	1,372,995
12	1,372,995		13,855	1,251,143
13	1,251,143		14,409	1,117,914
14	1,117,914		14,985	1,013,142
15	$1,013,142		$15,585	$ 892,212

*Emergencies

The ISRA recipient continues on in this fashion for all remaining years. Remember, withdrawals can be adjusted at the first day of any new year. For instance, if in the fifteenth year a retiree decides to conserve because there will be no need for that sum each year, the person can take out any amount desired, provided that the total annual withdrawal is less than the maximum. Let's say the person only wanted to withdraw $9,000 per month, rather than the $15,585 that could be taken. This would make the fund balance at the end of the fifteenth year $977,553, saving more than $85,000 that year. The option to change is always available.

If your spouse has a similar plan, then life will be pretty nice, financially, in your retirement years. It will also ease the tremendous burden of health care.

When a person dies, the balance of their ISRA fund would be passed on to their designated heirs, either in a lump sum or in monthly payments, as the heir so desires. This transfer of funds will happen when any ISRA participant dies, whether or not the individual has retired. This balance will be considered part of the estate and taxed according to current laws. If it is taken out in monthly payments then it will be taxed accordingly and not in one lump sum. In this way the surviving spouse and any children could be taken care of. This provision will act like the amendment to the Social Security Act passed in 1939, which extended monthly benefits to workers' dependents and survivors. It will also supplement the provisions for Death Benefits as provided for by the Social Security Act. These benefits are paid to survivors of workers who die from work injury. For example, a worker who dies after ten years would leave his family $45,138 (see the table on page 213). In addition, to provide for the family of any worker who dies before the seventeenth year of contributions to his ISRA, the worker will be insured to this seventeenth year through the SSIBC. In this example the family would receive an additional $75,120 from insurance. Payments will be made monthly for a reasonable period of years. The same insurance will apply to disabled workers also. They will be insured through the seventeenth year and paid monthly for ten years.

As was noted before, each individual may choose when he or she retires, with the earliest retirement age being fifty-five. Looking at the table we can see that retiring at age fifty-five means that the person will have worked, under normal conditions, thirty-five years. This will give the worker a fund balance of approximately $796,901. This of course will be different if the person had a greater amount withheld during his or her working years.

At this age, assuming you were the retiree, you can expect to live another twenty-five to thirty years, which would result in a monthly payout of approximately $2,200. This illustration will also apply to those who reach sixty-five, not having worked continuously. At age fifty-five, the monthly income is significantly less than it would be at age sixty-five, but other factors can enter into the final trust amount: increased funding on a voluntary basis (shown on p. 203) or a spouse retiring.

The only firm restriction to be put on the ISRA fund is that it will be treated as the current Social Security is now. You cannot touch the fund in any way until retirement. This includes borrowing against your fund.

All working men and women, including the self-employed, who now have FICA withheld, will continue these deductions by law, in the same manner. All workers under the age of thirty-seven would come under the ISRA program. All persons from ages thirty-seven to forty-five would have the option of the ISRA plan or staying with the current Social Security program. All workers who have not been under the current Social Security program will now also have the option of joining the ISRA program, using the same criteria.

The reason for these breaking points is fairly obvious. It is unlikely that anyone over forty-six could accrue a sufficient ISRA fund balance to take care of them by the time they reach retirement age. However, even at this late point an option can be set up for those over forty-six who wish to enter the ISRA plan. They would have to sign away any right to this Social Security account. Each person in this situation will have to decide which plan gives them the better financial outcome.

Once under the ISRA program no participant who shifts from Social Security can ever go back to the old program. The choice must rest with each individual.

Investing for the future has been done by countless people and companies for hundreds of years. Market forces will dictate the results. They are bound to have both good and bad periods, but over the decades this ISRA program will cover, long-term growth should continue.

16

Funding Current Social Security

"The struggle of today is not altogether for today, it is for a vast future, also."

Abraham Lincoln, 1861

The elderly and their retirement have become one of the most glowing examples of our desire to do what is right. At the same time it has also become a source of considerable exasperation. Michael J. Boskin wrote in his book *Too Many Promises,* "If the surplus in Social Security that is expected to accumulate and grow is dissipated and/or reforms to slow the growth of benefits and place Social Security on a more sound long-term financial footing are ignored, the financial schism between generations will worsen. Taxes will be pushed onto future generations of workers. The national saving rate will decrease as the Trust Fund dissipates, resulting in less available capital to finance investment, to increase productivity, and to raise future standards of living." Peter J. Ferrera echoed this thinking in his book *Social Security: Prospects for Real Reform*: "Over the years, the program has become surrounded by a cloak of demagoguery and misinformation, woven by political leaders and interest groups seeking to further their own ends. If the public is ever to support real Social Security reform, this cloak must be removed."

Rena Pederson, Vice President and Editorial Page Editor of the *Dallas Morning News,* put it this way in an article on October 1, 1995: "Privatize Social Security. Our system is robbing Paul, Jr., to pay Paul, Sr. Chile has proved privatization works. Its workers can opt out of the old system and invest in regulated pension funds. Those funds are growing at 13 percent a year, enriching Chileans and stimulating the economy. No wonder other countries, like Argentina, Australia, Sweden, are joining in. What are we waiting for?"

Privatization of Social Security has been written about and discussed by many, but all have come to the conclusion that it would not be possible because it would tax the current generation twice for the same thing, once through the normal payroll tax deduction and then by increasing taxes to pay for the special bonds that have accumulated in the trust funds as a result of Congress borrowing all the surplus through the years. But if vast changes aren't made in the near future, we will shift a huge tax burden onto the younger generation. They will not only be paying for the Social Security needs of current recipients but paying to accumulate for their own retirement. Huge increases will be needed to satisfy a system that is fast becoming insatiable.

Senator Kerrey (D-Neb.) in June 1994 was one of the few Democrats to admit that the current system is no longer sustainable. Unfortunately most people today are still looking to the government for answers. This must change since America's real wealth lies in individual growth and prosperity. Government has no wealth, and regressive tax policies do little to stimulate growth. Its taxing policies deter savings and investment, which are the real base of our economy.

There is an excellent way to change all this. Regardless of how actuaries, accountants, or economists crunch the numbers, the system now has the ability to be privatized completely without causing any hardship on either the young or the old. The current work force will not have to be overburdened and the elderly can rest easy knowing their current benefits are and always will be protected. The current system would then provide businesses with a tax saving opportunity they have never had before. Giving back $169 billion per year to business when the system is fully phased in will develop more new job opportunities than the government could ever accomplish. And to top it all off, forgiving the government's $400 billion debt to Social Security would be one huge step toward federal budget balancing. Then too, the workers of America would not have to see their taxes go up to pay for this debt.

While this can be done, as we've seen in Texas, more and more people are coming to realize that any new retirement system has to be set up so that it is no longer affected by the whims of Congress and/or the administration. Second, it must be fair to both the young and the old so that no group of taxpayers and workers are paying any more than the 6.2 percent they are now paying into the system. While Congress will no longer run this new system, it must be written into law that all workers and businesses will continue to pay the FICA tax as they are now through the normal withholding. Why? While this new approach focuses on the individual's choices regarding how to manage retirement nest eggs, the fact remains that most people will not save an adequate amount of their income unless required by law.

Over a decade ago Texas' down-to-earth Republican Congressman Bill Archer foretold this in a letter to me dated January 20, 1982. In part it read, "The major problem with all of the proposals to phase out Social Security is how you continue to pay benefits to those currently retired or over age forty. All current tax revenues are going to fund current benefits and either the FICA would have to be continued or general tax revenues would have to be used to pay the billions of dollars of currently unfunded benefits. Since continuing the FICA tax would undermine the ability of people to fully fund alternative IRAs and since there is no money from general tax revenues in a federal budget already heavily in deficit, the alternatives again appear limited." Congressman Archer's letter illustrated that the Congress of the eighties was still thinking from day to day and not planning for the future.

There are those who feel that today's senior citizens have paid their dues in the form of FICA taxes for all their working years. Others agree that this is true, but insist that means testing should now be applied to determine the level of benefits obtained if we are to recognize Social Security as a vehicle to help the less fortunate. Frankly, both have valid arguments and both are right. The only way to resolve this dilemma is to lay out both solutions and see which is the best for all.

First, the 6.2 percent now being contributed by all employers, even those whose employees elect the Individual Security Retirement Account program (ISRA), will continue to be withheld. These mandated funds will be used to help finance the present recipients (retirees) of Social Security. This includes the employer share of withholding for all new employees entering the work force and the ISRA system until the current system winds down to zero. The normal 6.2 percent in FICA taxes withheld from all workers staying in the current system will also be withheld in the usual manner. The current system will be administered by the Social Security Investment Banking System (SSIBC). All additional money will be provided as shown in tables 1 and 2. In this way no additional money will be needed from the general revenues of the federal government.

When any of the workers under the present Social Security program decide to retire and claim their benefits they will be governed by the current rules and regulations. Those under the new ISRA system will be governed according to that program.

There are two ways of taking Social Security and retirement for the working people of these United States into the twenty first century.

One way will benefit the workers and retirees, the private sector, all Americans through reduced taxes, and even the government (its IOUs will be ripped up). The second solution will just benefit the retirees, those who will remain under the current system and the younger generations. The first of these two solutions includes a modified means-testing program for all those workers retiring under the current system.

A survey done by the National Taxpayers Union Foundation (NTUF) in September 1993 revealed that many Americans would be willing to accept measures that would cut back on government programs once seen as untouchable. Seven in ten favor reducing benefits to high-income people receiving Social Security, a proportion which is seven percentage points higher than the year before, and most agree that the costs of these programs are not under control. The NTUF is a top-notch organization with an outstanding reputation, yet Congress seems to take no notice of its findings.

The Concord Coalition, a Washington-based organization, founded by former senators Warren Rudman and Paul Tsongas, and also Peter G. Peterson, to reduce and then eliminate the federal deficit (not to be confused with the National Debt), has also advocated and strongly supported means testing. In fact their 1994 survey found that 63 percent of those asked supported this idea. In the summer 1994 issue of the *Concord Courier,* the coalition's quarterly newsletter, it was reported that House Majority Leader Richard Gephart (D-Mo.) promised that significant entitlement reform would be considered by the House before the August recess. As it turned out this was the same old smoke and mirrors game. (Congressman Gephart lost his majority leadership courtesy of the American voters.) This article goes on to say that the House would consider means testing programs that would save some $200 billion between now and the year 2000, which tends to validate the adjustments found in table 1.

Table 1 explains how the funds needed will be obtained for solution No. 1.

Table 1

SOLUTION NO. 1

(all amounts are in billions)

	1995	1996	1997	1998–
Social Security expenditures	$339.0	358.0	377.0	398.0 (A)
Modified adjustments	–33.7	–36.8	–36.6	–39.7 (B)
	305.3	322.8	340.4	358.3
Funding—				
Business share of FICA	$174.4	184.6	194.9	205.4 (C)
Workers remaining in system	130.9	138.2	145.5	152.9 (D)
	$305.3	322.8	340.4	358.3

The funds for current recipients will be deposited in the SSIBC and invested in accordance with the rules and regulations of the new investment banking system. All current regulations for the present system will apply to disbursements.

Note the following: (A) Social Security expenditures are taken from the Congressional Research Service (CRS) Report 94-27 EPW, dated May 10, 1994, and include only the benefits portion of the expense.

(B): Upon retirement, all those with incomes over a certain level will have their Social Security benefits adjusted as indicated:

INCOME	REDUCTION
from $60,000 to $69,999	40%
to $79,999	50%
to $89,999	60%
to $99,999	70%
and over	80%

Each year the Internal Revenue Service will certify the incomes of all seniors earning over the dollar amounts listed to the SSIBC. For this purpose the only criteria will be Adjusted Gross Income on the Income Tax return. Remember, this indexing is a finite problem and will come to an end with the last of the recipients under the current system.

(C): For the base year of 1995, the Social Security funds generated will be approximately $368.8 billion, excluding interest. Of this, the matching portion from business will be $184.4 billion. Of this latter amount, $174.4 billion will be needed to fully fund the system. The balance (ten billion dollars) will be returned to the business community in the form of a tax adjustment. In succeeding years the surplus will gradually grow higher, and after adjusting for the annual fund requirement, the board of governors will review this and set the new rate for the coming year, so that in effect the excess funds will be returned to the private sector in the form of lower taxes, thus increasing the net profits for business. In this way they can put this money to work and provide thousands of new jobs and the industrial base will grow.

(D): The employees share will go into the system to provide funds for current recipients, as is done now.

As was outlined in the previous chapter, all those over age thirty-six will stay in the current Social Security system, unless they plan to opt out. According to the Department of Labor's Bureau of Labor Statistics, the total work force in this country through August 1993, is as follows:

AGE	NUMBER	PERCENT OF POPULATION
Under 36 years of age	56,186,000	43%
Over 36 years of age	73,296,000	57%
Total work force	129,472,000	100%

Based on these figures the dollar share for the employees in fiscal 1995 (see Trustees Report, table 111.B3, page 178) who remain in the system will be $105.1 billion ($184.4 billion × 57% = $105.1 billion). This can fluctuate depending on those opting for the new system and the various types of workers. In addition, it is well known that the most productive financial years for a worker are between the ages of thirty-five and fifty-five. Therefore, to compensate for this, 14 percent will be added to the 57 percent to bring the FICA taxes for those remaining in the system into the proper balance. In this case, the 1995 workers balance will be $184.4 billion × 71 percent = $130.9 billion.

Through the years as the elder employees go into retirement or die, their contributions will no longer be in the system. Two things will compensate for this. First, there will be a natural progression to prime earnings years by the younger employees. Their employers will continue to pay the FICA tax on the incomes of these younger people. That share of FICA will grow larger through these prime years, thereby taking up the slack. Second, younger employees entering the system through the next several decades will also be receiving larger starting salaries and so their employers will continue to pay the corporate portion of these larger FICA taxes until the current system comes to a close. The 1994 Trustees Report on Social Security, table 11.H1, indicates that in twenty-five years there will be 80,657 young employees entering the system as opposed to 53,322 people reaching retirement age.

Let's turn now to the second solution to the Social Security crisis. It will help only retirees and no one else.

Table 2
SOLUTION NO. 2
(all amounts are in billions)

	1995	1996	1997	1998
Social Security Expenditures	$339.0	358.0	377.0	398.0 (E)
Funding—				
Business share of FICA—	$184.4	194.6	204.9	215.4 (F)
Workers remaining in system	130.9	138.2	145.5	152.9 (G)
From S.S. Trust Funds—	23.7	25.2	26.6	29.7 (H)
	$339.0	358.0	377.0	398.0

These funds for current recipients would also be deposited in the SSIBC and invested accordingly. All current regulations for the present system would apply as to disbursements, but investing would be done in the same way as the new system. In other words, there would be no buying of Treasury bonds. The money paid in to Social Security would not be used to mask the real budget deficit. This in itself is a plus.

Note the following: (E) Social Security expenditures are taken from the CRS Report 94-27 EPW, dated May 10, 1994, and include only the benefits portion of the expense.

(F): Please refer to (C) under the first solution. All facts are the same. Procedures and dollar figures are the same. Information is taken from the 1994 Trustees Report, table 111.B3, page 178.

(G): Please refer to (D) under the first solution. All facts, figures, and dollar amounts remain the same.

(H): Annually the board of governors will review the funds needed to pay the current retiree benefits. They will then advise Congress and the Treasury as to the amount needed from the bonds held by the Social Security Trust Funds for that fiscal year. Current interest on the bonds will be used first. Unused current interest only will be paid to the SSIBC and allocated to the insurance fund for survivors and the disabled. Interest income as stated in the 1994 Trustees Report, table 111.B3, page 178, is sufficient to cover the amounts needed.

Under this second solution the program will use the entire business portion of the FICA taxes for the foreseeable future and in this way prevent any return of funds to the private sector for years. It will require the government to pay part of the current interest due to the Social Security Trust Funds, which would normally be a paper transaction to accomplish full payment for current recipients. When the board of governors reviews the insurance fund annually it can also determine if any interest can be turned back to the Treasury. The SSIBC shall never take any more than is necessary to fund the current recipients and the insurance fund.

Of course, all current recipients, under solution two, will receive the maximum benefits due to them under the system regardless of income, under the guidelines of the current system.

It must be noted here that all figures obtained from CRS reports include the self-employed. Therefore, in both solutions the self-employed will continue to pay their share as though it were the business portion. The 6.2 percent will go into the SSIBC as with all other workers.

The choice of these two solutions to the problems facing the current Social Security system have within them the answer to a useful question: Isn't it better to create thousands upon thousands of new jobs annually, and in this way expand the economy to the betterment of all citizens and provide the government with a much greater tax revenue base, while trimming expenses by reducing the size of the government? The answer is obvious. One solution eliminates the need to use any of the interest and bonds in the Social Security Trust Funds because it uses the means of testing Social Security recipients to distribute only the FICA tax it collects from businesses each year while returning the growing surplus revenues (as each year's obligation decreases) to businesses in the form of tax credits. Or, should we pay Social Security benefits in the full amount to all, regardless of income, as they have paid their Social Security taxes (FICA) for all their working years?

It has been argued that workers who have paid FICA throughout their working years have an "implied compact" with the Social Security Administration to benefits regardless of their economic circumstances at the time of retirement. This compact had no promises stating that those who didn't succeed in life had more of a right to claim benefits than those who did. It is further argued that means testing would weaken the primary reason for the general support of the program by the public, that people believe they have paid for their benefits and are not receiving a handout. This, however, is a doubtful argument since it would apply to only a small group of recipients. Then, too, it is said that means testing would discourage workers from saving or developing income-generating assets because it could disqualify them from receiving Social Security benefits. Perhaps this last argument is no longer valid since Congress has seen fit to tax Social Security benefits rather substantially now in connection with other income.

In chapter 3 there is a copy of the original Social Security brochure put out in 1936 by the then Social Security Board, which was independent. It does say, "The checks will come to you as a right. You will get them regardless of the amount of property or income you may have. If you prefer to keep on working after you are sixty-five, the monthly checks from the government will begin coming to you whenever you decide to retire." It does not say that if you earn more than a certain amount between ages sixty-two to seventy that you will be penalized. It does not say that after age seventy you may earn what you can and still receive all your benefits. It does not say you can retire at age sixty-two. It does not tell you how much retired workers in 1994 will receive. Congress has made these changes over the years, just as it added the concept of COLAs.

To argue that a man making over $60,000 per year needs another $1,000 plus per month to live up to a certain level would not sit well with 95 percent of the American people, for whom this brilliant idea was conceived and established. Second, under the current tax laws part of this Social Security income would be consumed as income tax before a person could spend it.

The need of society to redistribute resources should be based on the premise of equal opportunity for all. But to be fair, if a person does not wish to avail herself of today's countless opportunities, which is that person's right and privilege, does this mean society has to take care of her "from the womb to the tomb" (a tongue-in-cheek remark of the Lyndon Johnson era)? Remember, in addition to giving us an income in our retirement years, Social Security helps in ways of which we are seldom aware (recall the disability and widows and orphans provisions of Social Security).

The modified means-testing discussed earlier is just one more way we can all do our part. It will help tremendously in bringing Social Security up to date, to solve the problems looming on the horizon before they get out of hand and cause huge tax burdens in the future.

A window of opportunity has arrived that gives us a chance to do this right and no one, from the young to the elderly, will be penalized. Under the new Individual Security Retirement Account plan no one will pay FICA taxes twice, which has been a concern for many folks inside the beltway.

No one will lose a cent. We can be thankful that while they didn't recognize what they were setting up in 1984, Congress put into place the tools and programs to make this transition to a new and updated system in place. For this we can say thanks.

As to the notion that the lower end of the wage scale would not benefit from the ISRA concept one need only review chapter 15. A busboy or server in Texas would receive a sound retirement when he or she reaches age sixty-five. By starting the ISRA early in one's working career, the payments add up and accumulate compound interest tax-free over time. This idea alone could very well make many people consider working rather than taking welfare, and it is the work ethic that must be restored in people if today's problems are to be solved.

It has been noted that many people these days are living well beyond their normal life expectancy. At the end of the example in the previous chapter there still remain sufficient assets, in fact they continue to grow, to provide for the retiree for the balance of the individual's life. If it is felt that life expectancy after retirement is not the figure to use, then a larger figure such as "life plus ten years" could very well be used.

In no way would there be a double burden on any taxpayer during the transition or even later in the ISRA program because the funds now are all in place. It is only a matter of setting up the new SSIBC system and running with it. This is why chapter 19 could not have been written ten years ago. Congress in its own way provided everything, but never put it into action. The hard-working people of Congress had all the pieces of the puzzle but never stood back to take a good look at what they had put in place to see how it all fit together.

It has been said there is nothing new under the sun, but there are many ways to refit the pieces, and in this case the Social Security system must be rearranged to take better care of the elderly in their retirement. The ISRA simply demonstrates a much better way for the good of all, workers and retirees as well as business and government.

In order to provide an even greater opportunity for a better future for those staying under the current system, the workers who continue under Social Security will also be allowed to save up to 10 percent more, and have it deducted from their salaries as the current FICA is. These funds will be identified as such by the employer, and remitted with the other FICA taxes in the normal way. An annual report will be furnished to each individual in the plan. This optional feature can be adjusted in writing only on the first day of any new year. These savings will be treated as Social Security funds and cannot be touched until the worker retires. For example, if a forty-year-old worker making $40,000 per year contributes an additional 2.5 percent per year, when he or she retires at age sixty-five, an additional $75,000 will be available tax free. In this case he or she may receive it in a lump sum or in monthly payments, however the person wishes.

These savings will never be taxed when an individual retires. This is also true of retirement funds, under the ISRA plan. Since the employee's own money, and not taxes, supports the person, there is no reason to tax it. It has been proved time and time again that raising taxes is really not the answer when people need help. With lower taxes people think in positive ways. They are more willing to spend, save, and invest, which keeps money in circulation. Economies grow strong under these types of conditions.

Remember also that this ISRA plan will not alter Medicare. The

1.45 percent deducted for Medicare will still be deducted from every worker and matched by the employer. Similarly the restructuring of Social Security as the ISRA plan will not alter welfare programs such as SSI and Food Stamps which do not come from Social Security taxes, but are part of the federal budget and receive appropriations from Congress each year.

If solution No. 1 is implemented, the decline in the number of Social Security recipients over the next decades will mean that the FICA amounts needed from the private sector will eventually reduce to zero. During this period the board of governors will meet annually to adjust downward the amount businesses and the self-employed have to pay into the system, until funding is no longer needed. When this system is fully set up and operating, the board of governors can then close out the Social Security part of the current system by returning all these billions of dollars in special bonds marked canceled to the Treasury and write off any and all interest due.

In this way the American people can thank President Franklin D. Roosevelt for a wonderful idea that helped out millions over the years. What a great way to close out a system that has done so much for so many. This type of event has seldom happened in any government, and will show that America is ready for the new century and all the challenges that lie ahead of us.

All this can be done through the new Social Security Investment Banking Corporation. This system itself will be the key and the cornerstone, as we have said, will be the Individual Security Retirement Account. Both will be fully explained and outlined in greater detail in the next two chapters.

If Congress does not do what is expected and put a system like this into place, the natural laws of economics will come into play. After the year 2002, according to the 1994 Trustees Report, the actual cash expended to meet the claims of current recipients will exceed the actual revenues received. Then what will Congress and the administration do? They will no longer have a surplus to help hide the annual budget deficit. In fact they will have to start appropriating funds from general tax revenues to cover the amounts due to Social Security recipients.

The chart below shows the Social Security income and outgo as reported in the 1994 Trustees Report.

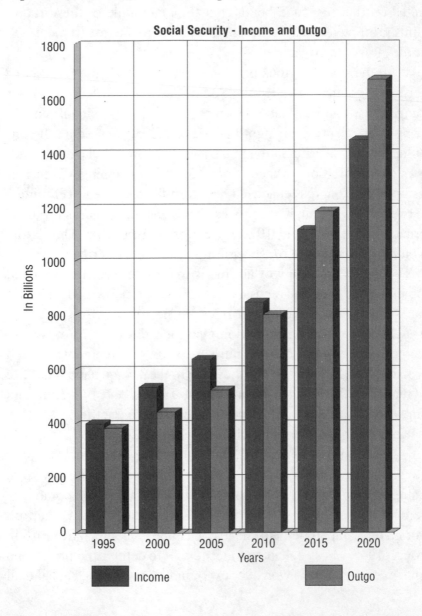

Social Security claims will start to exceed the system's income in approximately fifteen years. Some economists even say this will happen in only ten years. In fact, the Congressional Research Service report dated July 2, 1993, says, "The government has never defaulted on the trust fund bonds, but the magnitude of these future claims prompted many observers to ask where the government will get the money to cover them?"

Then there is a curious phenomenon that few Americans have ever heard about. It's called the Social Security "Notch." This is a strange twist that came about as a result of Congressional maneuvering over twenty years ago. In 1972 Congress passed a bill containing a huge miscalculation that essentially provided a double adjustment for inflation for many Social Security recipients. To correct this, in 1977 Congress enacted a new formula designed to eliminate the excess benefit, but in the process it reduced the benefits for those born between 1917 and 1921 by almost ten percent. This is the "Notch," or black hole for several million older Americans.

The deplorable irony of all this is that these were the men and women who fought, and thousands of whose comrades died, in World War II to preserve liberty and freedom not only in America, but throughout the world. And in doing so their lives and futures were changed forever. They paid the ultimate price, with their courage and heroism, from Europe and North Africa to the savage baptism of fire at Guadalcanal, through the horrors of Tarawa and Iwo Jima and many other Japanese-held islands in the Western Pacific.

Ken Shaub, now a senior citizen living in Houston, Texas, is of that generation. As a young, twenty-three-year-old corporal, along with tens of thousands of other marines of the 4th Marine Division, he slugged and fought his way onto the blood-stained and bomb ravaged beaches of Roi Namur in the Kwajalein Islands, then on through other Japanese-held islands of Tinian and Saipan, from 1943 through 1945. These gallant marines fought to defend and protect the rights of all Americans won over two hundred years ago. Ken and all these fine young Americans did it for love of country without concerns about financial rewards in the future, but this has long been forgotten.

Some lawmakers say that there is really nothing to raise their voices about. According to Congress, these men and women, many of whom are veterans are receiving a decent Social Security check each month. But are they really? Others simply say that this generation is passing into the history books. But let us all remember: they are still here, fewer in number, but still here, and they should not be forgotten.

Many in Congress have tried to correct this problem in order to be fair to all, but very little has ever been done. In point of fact nothing has been done. According to the National Committee to Preserve Social Security, it will cost just over $4 billion a year to correct this disparity of payments, an amount that will dwindle as the years go by. The ISRA program could correct this injustice since the interest on funds deposited with the SSIBC will generate more than enough surplus to repay the lost monies.

17

The Social Security Investment Banking Corporation

"The originative part of America, the part of America that makes new enterprises, that part into which the ambitious and gifted workingman makes his way up, the class that saves, that plans, that organizes, that presently spreads its enterprises until they have national scope and character, that middle class is being more and more squeezed out by the processes which we have been taught to call prosperity."

Woodrow Wilson, 1912

And so it is with this great institution called Social Security. Through thoughtless Congressional action (and inaction), or perhaps we should say shortsightedness, its use of the trust funds is squeezing the future of this great idea. With the continuing questionable adjustments being made, such as COLAs, they are putting tremendous pressures on the system, which were never dreamed of at its inception. As had been said, COLAs are great for the recipients but are an increasing burden on the budget and the single most important reason for its continuing growth. It is a double-edged sword.

There is only one way to put an end to such inappropriate use of funds intended for the retirement of the working men and women of this country. We the people must take the system out of the hands of politicians and reconstitute it into a system designed for retirement purposes, and accountable only to the people it serves, America's working people. The tremendous growth of this country is due in large part to the willingness of its people to stand on their collective feet and forge ahead with new ideas.

The basic outline and structure for this new investment banking corporation system is as follows:

1. It shall be called, "THE SOCIAL SECURITY INVESTMENT BANKING CORPORATION."

2. This investment banking corporation will be set up, have the characteristics of, and be a combination of both a large mutual fund and the Federal Reserve Banking System. The United States, including Alaska and Hawaii, will be divided into twelve districts, with branches in various cities within each district. The headquarters district for this investment banking corporation will be the eleventh district and the headquarters bank will be in Dallas, Texas. The reason for this is that the SSIBC is not a government entity. It has been designed to handle the future retirement for millions of working Americans and a new setting is needed, one that will give people and new ideas room to flower and grow.

3. The Social Security Investment Banking Corporation (SSIBC) will be a quasi-governmental entity that combines private and governmental features, mandatory and voluntary features. These special features will be explained and discussed as we go. This system will be privately owned and operated. In the initial start-up phase the president, with the advice and consent of the Senate, will appoint the governing body that will serve for an initial two-year term only.

This temporary start up is necessary since the SSIBC will have to become established, stock issued and sold, and the voting structure has to be worked out. It will be the task of this board of governors to set things in motion. The board will consist of seven directors, one being the chairman. They will be appointed by the president and confirmed by the Senate.

The following illustration outlines this basic concept.

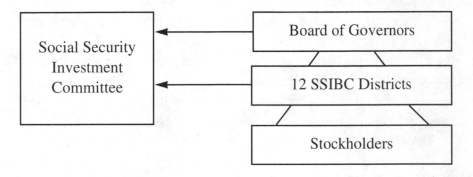

THE BOARD OF GOVERNORS

The top of the above pyramid consists of the Board of Governors. This board shall consist of seven members appointed by the president and confirmed by the Senate for fourteen-year terms, with one new member appointed every two years. For the initial appointments of the first seven directors their terms will be staggered from two years through fourteen years. Thereafter the term for each new governor will be fourteen years. These terms will be nonrenewable. In addition, they cannot be removed by the president. This is designed to insulate the board from political pressures.

After the Senate has confirmed the nominees the names of the nominees will be submitted to the stockholders, the working people and retirees, for final approval, within six months of the end of the initial two year start up period. A simple majority will suffice. If anyone is not approved, the process will be repeated for those positions.

Once in office the governors are expected to make decisions in accordance with the regulations and the broad national interest. As with the Federal Reserve, the fourteen-year terms are staggered so that one governor's term expires and one new governor is appointed every two years. The initial full terms will be staggered accordingly. This feature ensures that no president can stack the board at one time.

The president also designates which of the seven governors will serve as the chairman of the board of governors. However, the four year term of the chairman will not coincide with the president's term of office. The chairman will serve only one four-year term. It will be further stipulated that only one member of the board of governors may be selected from each of the twelve districts at any one time.

THE SOCIAL SECURITY INVESTMENT BANK DISTRICTS

The center of the pyramid consists of the twelve district Social Security Investment Banks: one headquarters bank, which I have located in Dallas, Texas, and eleven other banks, one for each district. All of these investment banks will be private corporate entities that together compose the SSIBC and service Individual Security Retirement Accounts throughout the United States.

The general operations of these twelve districts will be broadly supervised by the board of governors, but their day-to-day investment and banking activities will be largely independent of board involvement. Moreover, they will function as autonomous institutions relative to each other.

Each district will be managed by a nine-member board of directors that will be both appointed and elected, six of whom must be nonbankers. Directors of the District Investment Bank boards will be selected in two different ways. Three directors will be appointed by the board of governors and six directors will be elected by the people of each district who hold voting shares issued from that district, whether they live in the district or not. Each director will serve a three-year term that is nonrenewable, and terms will be staggered so that three are elected or appointed each year.

The chair and deputy chair of each District Investment Bank will appoint the president and the executive vice-president for the district by simple majority vote of the district board. The term of each president and executive vice-president shall be limited to one five year term for each district bank. These terms shall be nonrenewable. Salaries shall be no more than twice the salaries for similar positions at the Federal Reserve Banks.

The president of each District Investment Bank, with the approval of the board of directors of the district, shall appoint an executive vice-president to be in charge, and operate each branch investment bank, under the guidelines of the district president and the board of directors of the district. The branch executive vice president will serve at the discretion of the district president, but for no more than five years.

The twelve Social Security Investment Banks and their branches are profit-making entities, and the profits will be credited to all Individual Security Retirement Accounts at the end of each fiscal year. Operating expenses will be covered and the funding of this new private investment banking system shall come from service charges and investment fees. These charges and fees shall total no more than $5 per year per account. The board of directors of each district shall have the authority to reduce these charges each year if the funds are not needed. No surplus shall ever be accumulated for operations, nor shall there ever be a deficit.

THE STOCKHOLDERS

At the base of the pyramid are the stockholders, the foundation of this system, which in reality are the working men and women of these United States. What better foundation could there be? These are the average, ordinary, everyday working people who for generations have been the foundation all of the giant industries in America: e.g., ship building, steel making, automobile manufacturing, and many others. It is now time to turn this retirement system over to the people who have earned the right to determine their own future. As stockholders they will have the final say on any and all changes to this system once it is set up and operating. (For details see chapter 18.)

A key part of this pyramid is the twelve-member National Social Security Investment Committee, which will establish the investment policy for the SSIBC. It will consist of the seven governors, the president of the Dallas headquarters investment bank, and four other district presidents. This committee will be responsible for setting general investment policy guidelines and to see that the twelve districts invest the funds properly, according to specific guidelines. The day-to-day investment operations will be handled by each district investment bank.

Initially the funding for the Social Security Investment Banking Corporation will be in the form of a loan from the government which shall be repaid, in full, plus normal interest, within five years. The amount needed will depend in large part upon the amount received from the sale of stock in the SSIBC to all eligible people. The only requirement for eligibility will be that the stock purchasers must have paid or be paying Social Security taxes (FICA). In other words, those people who have worked and those who are working, even on a part-time basis, may purchase stock. Work is the key word. (This will be discussed further in chapter 18 also.)

With the Resolution Trust Corporation holding many buildings and properties from failed banks and savings and loans, there should be no trouble in finding the necessary facilities. Wherever possible the Social Security Investment Banking Corporation shall buy and own its buildings.

The Social Security Investment Banking Corporation will have four reasons for its existence.

1. The first reason is to collect the funds withheld by employers from each employee and to credit such amounts to the individual retirement account of each worker. The funds will actually be deposited by each company or self-employed individual in the same manner or fashion as all companies and individuals do today. Quarterly estimates will be paid into the system as they are today. If the funds are not received from the private sector in a timely fashion, the same penalties and interest will apply as under the present system. The proceeds from these penalties will also be remitted to the SSIBC. Enforcement procedures will remain as they are today. Quarterly reports, such as the current form 941 and annual reconciliation will be required of all companies, as they are now.

2. The second function of the SSIBC is to invest funds received in safe and sound investments such as Blue Chip stocks, sound mutual funds, high grade bonds, and government treasury notes and bonds. Only those government issues that are sold to the public will be allowed. Rules and regulations will be very strict on the quality of all investments. In addition, no more than 20 percent of the stock of any company may be purchased or owned by the SSIBC. This will prevent the bank from gaining controlling interest in any of the various companies in which it invests. Investment managers, as with any mutual fund, will make these investment decisions, free from any government pressures.

The SSIBC will also have the right to make interest-bearing loans to federal, state, and local governments. In the aggregate, all such loans, in total, to the various governmental bodies, will never exceed five percent of the total portfolio. Outstanding loans must be paid in full before any additional loans may be made to a particular governmental body. All loans must have proper security and safeguards. No funds will ever be invested in derivatives under any circumstances.* This type of investment caused many problems for state and local pension plans as well as numerous governmental bodies. Orange County, California, serves as a particularly tragic example of this problem and its aftermath. Additional examples of these problems have already been discussed in chapter 11.

3. The SSIBC's third function is to dispense the monthly retirement checks to all retirees and then to those who fall under the current system. In the years to come the retirement benefits will be dispensed as outlined in previous chapters.

Once a year the Social Security Investment Banking Corporation will be required to furnish an income, interest, and withdrawal statement to each person who has funds in the SSIBC banks. A statement will also be sent to all those under the current Social Security system showing the COLA increases for the coming year.

4. The SSIBC is to collect FICA taxes and make payments to all working men and women who retire and who are now retired under the current Social Security system, until this function is completed. The funds that are withheld (FICA) from employees who stay in the current system will remain the same as they are today, 6.2 percent. This percentage will never increase, but the maximum wages for deduction will follow current regulations. The corporate portion of FICA is also added to the employees' percentage. These funds will be invested as all other funds received, so that they will generate the additional income needed to take care of the cost-of-living adjustments. The income generated by these funds and monies dispensed to individual retirees will always be tax free.

The Social Security Investment Committee is the investment policy decision making center. Its center of operations will be in the

---

*Derivatives are speculations by stockbrokers.

headquarters branch in Dallas, Texas. This committee will be in overall charge of how all the funds received are invested. The members will establish the general guidelines for the twelve districts, and will consistently monitor the investments made to see that the guidelines are followed. Day-to-day responsibility for the various investments will be in the hands of the portfolio managers and their staffs who are, experts in their fields, similar to those working with large mutual funds.

It has already been mentioned that the Social Security Investment Committee will have twelve members, among them the seven members of the board of governors, the president of the Dallas headquarters branch, and four of the eleven district investment bank presidents. The four bank presidents, who will serve one-year terms, will be selected in rotation from the four remaining regional clusters. No investment bank president shall be eligible to repeat his or her membership on the committee until all other presidents in the cluster have served. The five regional clusters shall be as follows: (1) Dallas; (2) Boston, New York, Philadelphia; (3) Cleveland, Richmond, Atlanta; (4) Chicago, Minneapolis, St. Louis; (5) Kansas City, San Francisco.

These twelve districts will be separate entities and will freely compete with each other much like the divisions of major corporations compete. Each district will be charged with getting the best return for its investors (i.e., the working people of this country) in its district. Districts may never vote as a block with other districts on any companies in which they share an investment interest.

This investment function is the most important part of the new system, and with the huge sums of money that will be in play, temptations are bound to arise, and so, a very strong, independent auditing system will need to be put in place to review and monitor on an annual basis the operations of the twelve districts and their branches. This auditing division shall be the direct responsibility of the board of governors. The annual report of the auditors will be delivered to the board and sent to all stockholders within four months after the close of each fiscal year. An annual independent audit will also be done to confirm such findings at the end of each fiscal year and will be distributed to all concerned parties. Spot audits will also be done every six months and the results will be reported to the Board of Governors for review and any action necessary.

The map below shows each district.

Each Social Security Investment Banking Corporation district shall have the following branch territories, as shown on the map:

1. Boston

2. New York, Buffalo

3. Philadelphia

4. Cleveland, Pittsburgh, Cincinnati

5. Richmond, Baltimore, Charlotte

6. Atlanta, Nashville, Birmingham, New Orleans, Jacksonville, Miami

7. Chicago, Detroit

8. St. Louis, Louisville, Memphis, Little Rock

9. Minneapolis, Helena

10. Kansas City, Omaha, Denver, Oklahoma City

11. Dallas, Houston, San Antonio, El Paso

12. San Francisco, Los Angeles, Portland, Seattle, Salt Lake City

I have designated Dallas to be the headquarters of this new system for a number of reasons. There must be a complete separation from Congress and the federal government. The SSIBC's purpose is purely to serve a retirement function and should focus only on that effort, without the added complication of a political environment, as would be found in Washington, D.C.

Finally, the board of governors shall not have the authority to alter the number of districts unless authorized by a vote of all the stockholders. The governors may change or adjust lines within a district and add additional branches to accommodate natural changes in population centers or to improve operating efficiency. To do this at least five of the seven governors must concur, and then approval must be given by the stockholders. With today's high-speed computers and the information network, such votes needed for approval of new branches can be handled expeditiously.

18

Public Ownership of the SSIBC

"And to preserve their independence, we must not let our rulers load us with perpetual debt. We must make our election between economy and liberty, or profusion and servitude."

Thomas Jefferson, 1816

For years Congress refrained from making any sound decisions concerning the ever-growing deficit, and for us that is the reason Social Security's financial problems have kept mounting right along with the national debt. The government's efforts to convince the American people that all was well continued working for many decades after World War II, but things began to turn in the nineties. The politicians inside the beltway thought average citizens would believe anything Capitol Hill chose to tell them. But the truth of the matter is that average workers really do know what is going on. And that proved to be the downfall of many in Congress.

247

It is time to set up a modern system for the twenty-first century that will give back to the workers the right to take charge of their own future and all that goes with it. For the past sixty years this system has helped millions of elderly and retired workers and for this the architects of Social Security can be justifiably proud. But in its current overburdened and underfinanced form, its days are numbered. In part this book has been an attempt to outline the demise of the Social Security system if it maintains its present course.

The new concept and system called the SSIBC is desperately needed in order to give everyone a fair deal and to fulfill the promise of retirement that millions have worked for all their lives.

What the people of this country need is a government that will respond to the needs of its citizens. We need a government that will give Americans a pat on the back for taking care of themselves rather than socking them with additional taxes because they tried to do so.

This Social Security Investment Banking Corporation (SSIBC) will be a retirement system for all working and retired people, and in all fairness the workers should be given a chance to own the system and to participate equally. Initially the stock of the SSIBC will be offered to all those paying FICA (Social Security) taxes or who have retired on Social Security. In the future it would be offered as a right when a person opens an Individual Security Retirement Account, i.e., when FICA taxes are first withheld. In the future the term FICA taxes will be phased out in favor of ISRA withholding, which will be appropriate since it will no longer be a regressive tax, but an investment in the worker's future. There will also be a very key difference between the two functions. When FICA taxes are withheld it is a tax pure and simple and is gone forever. The worker has no claim on the Social Security taxes other than a hopeful promise from Congress that a monthly benefit will be paid upon reaching sixty-five. So long as the money withheld remains a tax it is a promise Congress can change, either increase or decrease, at any time.

With the ISRA, workers have a specific amount of money invested in their future. That money is always theirs and cannot be taken away. Upon retirement the money is returned to the workers, in addition to all the accumulated interest and growth that has been the result of this investment. When the account owner dies the balance of the ISRA in the retirement fund goes to the decedent's heirs, in accordance with the estate. Under the ISRA withholding, if you were to die early in life, the entire balance would go to your heirs. With today's Social Security, your heirs only get a small monthly death benefit and a small monthly spousal benefit.

The SSIBC stock will be initially offered at $25 per share in the starting year. This is an arbitrary amount I selected, but it is sufficient to get the job done to start the system, yet small enough to be within most everyone's reach. In each succeeding year the purchase price will be increased by one dollar ($1) per year. Each working or retired individual will be allowed to buy up to, or own, one hundred (100) shares, and no more. The reason for this is straightforward and very simple. You do not want anyone to accumulate enough shares to have an effect on the system in any way, shape or form. Shares will never be sold to any private sector business of any kind, large or small, or any brokerage house or bank, at any time. This program is only for the individual working men and women of this country. Since the inception of retirement and pension plans, as well as Social Security the workers have been used and abused by both the public and private sectors. They have always come in second when there is any discussion of changes in any system. Through owning stock in SSIBC, workers can have a say in how the system is run.

Each person will be given an initial five-year period in which to purchase stock. It will be the right of each person to buy from one share to a hundred shares. Should any person not have the funds to buy stock immediately, provisions shall be made to allow the purchase over this five year period. For those who are minors at the commencement of the new program, a reasonable time will be allowed for the purchase of the stock, say, up to the age of thirty.

It should be noted that an individual *does not* have to buy any shares in the Social Security Investment Banking Corporation to have an Individual Security Retirement Account under the system. This will be the law and shall be done automatically with the first ISRA (remember, it's no longer FICA) deposit. In other words, you don't have to buy stock in General Motors in order to buy a Buick. But you do have to own stock to vote on board members, other elections, and any policy decisions put to a vote of stockholders.

If a person wishes to sell his or her shares, said shares will have to be sold back to the Social Security Investment Banking Corporation. The price for these shares will be the value at the time of the sale, but never less than the price each person originally paid for the stock. Shares could be inherited. If such an inheritance were to give a person more than the limit of a hundred shares, the additional shares would have to be sold back to the SSIBC at the current market price.

When we make a normal stock purchase it is done with the expectation of capital gain and income. In this case, investing in the Social Security Investment Banking System is done for control of, and a say in, the corporation that will be investing your money for future growth to build your retirement. Stock purchasers will have all the rights of any stockholder in any corporation, and more. In this case, those owning stock will have the final say in the selection of the board of governors for the overall system and selection of the board of directors for the district where the person's funds are kept. In this way Congress and the administration can no longer pick someone the public has doubts about to run a major national retirement system. Each person owning stock will be entitled to one vote for each share owned, and will be entitled to vote on any and all matters pertaining to the SSIBC. Ninety days, at least, must be provided to all stockholders to vote on all matters presented.

Dividends will be paid on these shares on an annual basis. The board of directors of each district will review the profit and loss statements of their district on an annual basis, to declare the amounts to be paid. Dividends will be credited to each individual's ISRA account, and a statement will be sent to each individual.

Any profit made on the sale of the SSIBC stock shall never be considered anything but taxable income, since the stock is not part of the retirement plan. Dividends on the other hand, credited to each account will always be tax free because the money is for retirement.

Information on each person's retirement account will be strictly confidential. No information shall ever be released to anyone, under any circumstances, including any branch of the government (federal, state, or local), or any business in the private sector for any reason, at any time. The IRS will not be permitted any information on these accounts and will be forbidden by law to place liens or attachments on ISRA funds. This will also hold true for any federal, state, or local court, as well as any business or individual.

The initial SSIBC stock offering should bring in over $100 billion. After all of the twelve districts and their branches have been set up and are operating, there should and will be more than ample funds to pay off, with interest, the initial loans received from the federal government. It shall be a direct mandate to the board of governors that they pay off these loans as soon as possible.

If necessary, this initial funding will also be used to pay the benefits of present recipients in the Social Security system, as detailed in chapter 17. These moneys will be replaced as soon as the system is fully operational.

It is essential to set up this independent banking and investment system as soon as possible to secure the future of all retirees. In order to insure the independence of the system, any changes necessary must be approved by two-thirds of both houses of Congress, agreed to by the president, and finally submitted to all the stockholders of the Social Security Investment Banking System for their approval. No change will be made until the stockholders give their approval. A simple majority is all that will be required. In this way the new system will be independent and the government can get out of the retirement business, and get on with running the country.

Upon retirement, after working forty-five years or so, a person should no longer have to worry about whether a pension or retirement plan is waiting to help in the years ahead. The SSIBC program will solve both the concerns of workers and those of businesses. Perhaps it will help instill the work ethic back in people who have long ago forgotten what it is to do a day's work and smile at the end of the day to know that they are standing on their own two feet and no longer in need of help from some government body. Workers in the SSIBC program will know that they are building their own future. And businesses will be relieved at not having to set up pension schemes for their workers.

Finally, government at all levels—federal, state, and local—will feel new vitality as never before, when the retirement of its employees is no longer an ever-growing responsibility. It will be a sight to see the downsizing of both private and public sector when all the bureaucracy is no longer needed. With these transformations the need for all the current taxes should diminish. Isn't it ironic that by getting a much better and sounder retirement system the people of this country should actually pay lower taxes!

It's a feeling no one has known in recent memory, and everyone should experience it at least once in a lifetime.

"Give a man the secure possession of a bleak rock, and he will turn it into a garden; give him a nine years' lease of a garden, and he will convert it into a desert. The magic of Property turns sand to gold."

Arthur Young, 1787

19

The Win-Win Results

"We are not primarily put on this earth to see through one another,
but to see one another through."

Peter De Vries

The fortunes of every working man and woman, whether we like it
or not, are inextricably linked to the destiny of Wall Street and the
markets. It's as though the stock market is serving as the heart,
pumping the financial lifeblood for the country's economic growth
and expansion. Since its inception in the early 1800s the wizards of
Wall Street have used the Stock Exchange to make and further their
fortunes. They have understood where the real money is made. For
over a hundred years, since the Industrial Revolution in the mid
1800s, the growth of the United States has been reflected in the ex-
changes and markets. The time has come to stop looking to the city
on the Potomac for retirement, and look instead to the financial cen-

ters for the monetary growth needed to bring a sound solution to the future retirement of the American worker.

Looking to private industry is also the wrong direction. Today's business can no longer afford the ever-growing cost of retirement. In 1994 and in 1995 we heard that business was good and profits were up, and yet big business continued to down-size and cut its labor costs. Oil companies, telephone companies, electronics giants, to name but a few, were all cutting back thousands of employees. Why? One of the private sector's largest expenses is the retirement packages it offers employees. Looked at realistically retirement is a never-ending cost that throws the profit and loss statement way out of balance. In some cases, older businesses could find themselves with more retirees than current employees!

For business to show a real rebirth in growth and profits this added financial burden will have to be eliminated. Fortunately, we are at a point in time where this can be done very successfully. There is only one sound answer now. Set up an Individual Security Retirement Account program for all workers and everyone wins. It relieves the private sector of a huge financial problem while at the same time ensuring each and every American worker a safe and sound pension plan that will provide for them in their elder years. This ISRA system will allow workers to act in concert with one another. No one will have to worry about all the functions, such as where to invest the money, keeping track of the progress of investments, or worrying about downturns. They will be part of a system whose job it is to do all this for them, and the system will always be there.

Not surprisingly our nation's leaders have already come to realize this. Chapter 11 vividly demonstrates how lawmakers have used a system similar to this ISRA program very successfully for all government employees under FERS, called the Thrift Savings Plan. It's time to give the American worker, the backbone of this country, the same chance at a secure future. In addition, free enterprise has conclusively shown that this new concept will work very successfully as demonstrated in Galveston, Brazoria, and Matagorda counties of south Texas.

At the same time the private sector, including the self-employed, will benefit as never before. Phasing out the employer's share of the Social Security tax will over time return to the business community more than $169.2 billion per year. In future years this figure could be even larger, reaching over $250 billion annually. Giving back to the private sector is almost unheard of these days, and may send chills up and down the spine of many of those inside the Washington beltway. Not having to pay these FICA taxes in future years will be a tremendous boon to the business climate.

As an example, a small company with three restaurants and one hundred employees would save over $100,000 per year—a tremendous amount for a small business. A medium size business, with some 2,500 employees, can save over three million dollars per year when this new ISRA program is completely phased in.

A letter I received from Larry N. Forehand, president of Casa Olé Mexican Restaurants in Texas, had this to say: "We currently pay over $1.3 million in matching Social Security taxes annually. If our company had that $1.3 million a year to invest in new locations, we could build six additional restaurants, employ an additional four hundred fifty people and add $7.2 million to the economy every year."

Large corporations, such as Chrysler Corporation, can save over two billion dollars per year, and a great deal more if they ponder the following question: If, as the employer, I know that all my employees will have a sound retirement (some with as much as one million dollars in their fund), why then would it be necessary to provide a company pension plan for the employees? Think of the astounding and untold effects this would have on business, profits, prices, unions, employees, and retirees!

In addition to the very large monetary benefit, many government rules and regulations may no longer be needed. Moreover, employees or retirees would no longer find it necessary to worry about the financial condition of their employer or what may happen to their pensions at large corporations when contract time rolls around. Businesses could then become much more competitive in both domestic and global markets.

Then, too, simply by securing the retirement of the average Jane and Joe, the federal government will be able to wipe out a half-trillion-dollar debt without raising taxes or cutting benefits. All this without adding another fifty thousand bureaucrats to the payroll and another cabinet department. Imagine it! The days of big government could start coming to an end.

With business receiving a greater net income because it doesn't have to support retirement plans, both the federal and state governments will benefit by receiving billions of dollars in additional corporate taxes. In the first year of this new system approximately $28 billion would be in the coffers of the private sector. This is net income and would generate new taxes in the amount of $8 billion to $10 billion. When the ISRA plan is fully phased in it would generate over $100 billion in new taxes. And remember, *this is being done with no tax increases to anyone!*

The federal government can then ask itself the same question that the business sector did: Why would it be necessary for the government to provide a second retirement system for its employees when it knows that all government employees will have a sound and safe retirement with the ISRA? The untold and beneficial effect this would have on the federal budget, the national debt, and the economy generally cannot be measured at this time. It will be in the hundreds of billions of dollars.

There are many examples to choose from. According to a Congressional Research Service (CRS) brief, the monies borrowed from the military trust fund alone account for over $90 billion of the federal debt in fiscal year 1993. In fiscal year 1991 the federal government paid out $32.8 billion in retirement benefits to government retirees, under its CSRS and FERS categories. These amounts will continue to increase in the years ahead. This is in accordance with another CRS brief from the Library of Congress. And the COLAs attached to these programs will grow even faster. This would also have a profound effect on the underfunded pension obligations of the federal government, which at last report (fiscal year 1993) were running over 1.5 trillion dollars.

In addition, various government payrolls can be reduced substantially. How many people now work administering the many federal pension plans and related benefit expenditures in the Office of Personnel Management (OPM) and the newly independent Social Security Agency? With the money saved when the ISRA plan is fully in place all nonretirement benefit functions could be put under one umbrella administrator, thereby eliminating the need for three or four departments to handle these functions.

The list goes on and on. The debt owed to the Social Security Trust Funds (at present nearly half a trillion dollars) can be eliminated within two years after the ISRA program is in place and running. The ISRA program will use only current funds and thus will have no need for what was appropriated by the U.S. Treasury over the past decade. This will also cancel out the billions of dollars of interest that would have had to be accrued and accounted for by the Treasury on these non-negotiable bonds. When was the last time that anyone gave back the federal government that much money?

Another side effect is that all fifty states could also opt for this type of Individual Security Retirement Account system, and get out of the retirement business, if they so desire. It would save them billions upon billions of dollars a year, yet they will know their employees are well taken care of.

The most important reason for the ISRA plan remains the secure retirement of the working men and women of America. This need cries out from the fifty-five-year-old middle-management executive who was let go because of down-sizing or merger, to the young, single parent who has no way of starting a retirement program with the burdens she must have. Both however, are forced to pay Social Security taxes, all the while wondering if they ever will see the benefits owed them. Both could expect a sound retirement under the new ISRA program.

No longer will workers worry and wonder about how much they will have at retirement. They will know: it will be tracked on their quarterly statements, and it will be free of outside political forces that have plagued retirees for so long. Workers' retirement will be set up in a government sponsored enterprise, but owned by the working people of America, in the Social Security Investment Banking Corporation.

It's time to act. It's time to get rid of Social Security as we know it, and take charge of the future.

For more information write:
The CRISS Coalition
Committee for *Real Independent* Social Security
P.O. Box 925673
Houston, Texas 77292

Glossary

AARP: American Association of Retired Persons. The largest senior advocacy group in the United States. It's headquartered in Washington, D.C.

AFDC: Aid to Families with Dependent Children. A government welfare program.

The Alternate Plan: Name of the Galveston, Texas, pension plan that was set up for county employees to replace Social Security, after the employees voted to opt out of Social Security.

Baby Boomers: Those men and women, born in the decade after World War II, who would now be in their forties. Estimates of their numbers run as high as eighty million.

CBO: Congressional Budget Office. The arm of Congress that estimates budgetary figures on proposed programs for Congress.

C Fund: One of the three funds of the Thrift Savings Plan for federal employees administered by the Federal Retirement Thrift Investment Board. The C Fund is invested primarily in a commingled Standard & Poor's 500 Stock index fund.

COLA: Cost-of living-adjustment. An annual adjustment written into law by Congress to provide yearly increases to retirees' benefits to compensate them for inflation. The rate of increase is based on the Consumer Price Index (see CPI).

Compounding: Interest computed on the sum of an original principal and accrued interest.

CPI: Consumer Price Index. An index measuring the change in the cost of typical wage-earner purchases of goods and services expressed as a percentage of the cost of these same goods and services in some base period.

CSRS: Civil Service Retirement System. The old government retirement system in use prior to January 1, 1994.

Entitlements: A term coined during Ronald Reagan's presidency to cover Social Security and welfare programs.

ERISA: The Employee Retirement Income Security Act of 1974, which was enacted to protect employees of private pensions through government insurance and regulations.

Fannie Maes: Interest-bearing bonds issued and backed by the Federal National Mortgage Association.

FERS: The Federal Employees Retirement System, effective January 1, 1984, to replace the older CSRS. This enabled Congress to include federal employees in the Social Security program.

F Fund: One of the three funds of the Thrift Savings Plan administered by the Federal Retirement Thrift Investment Board on behalf of federal employees. The F Fund is a bond index fund invested primarily in a commingled Shearson Lehman Hutton Government/Corporate bond index fund.

FICA: Federal Insurance Contributions Act, which authorized Social Security's payroll tax deductions.

G Fund: One of the three funds of the Thrift Savings Plan. A retirement plan for federal employees administered by the Federal Retirement Thrift Investment Board. The G Fund consists of investments in short-term, nonmarketable U.S. Treasury securities specially issued to the plan.

G.I. Bill: A government sponsored education bill for all United States armed forces from World War II in which the government paid most of the costs for these veterans to pursue their education.

Ginnie Mae: A certificate issued by the Government National Mortgage Association (GNMA), a U.S. government corporation within the Department of Housing and Urban Development. Specifically, a Ginnie Mae security represents part ownership in a pool of Federal Housing Administration (FHA)-insured and Veteran's Administration (VA)-guaranteed residential mortgages. GNMA fully guarantees timely payment of principal and interest.

Great Depression: An era of very hard times for the American people after the 1929 crash of the stock markets. This period is normally considered to be from 1930 to 1940.

House Ways and Means Committee: The committee of the U.S. House of Representatives that originates all tax bills and oversees the Social Security program.

Indexing: A term denoting annual increases by using a number to indicate change in magnitude, as of cost or price, as compared with annual increases.

ISRA: Individual Security Retirement Account. The new program designed to give every worker a sound retirement, free of government interference, and based on investment, compound interest, and time.

Means-testing: An examination into the financial state of a person to determine his or her eligibility for public assistance. Many think it should be used as a basis for Social Security benefits.

NCSSR: National Commission for Social Security Reform. A commission formed by President Reagan in 1981 to solve the then bankruptcy of Social Security.

New Deal: The name given to President Franklin Roosevelt's first two terms in office. It was during this period that many lasting programs and agencies were originated.

Notch: A name given to an inadvertent reduction of Social Security benefits by Congress for those retirees born from 1917 through 1921.

OASDI: Old-Age, Survivors, and Disability Insurance. This program is popularly referred to as Social Security.

PBGC: The Pension Benefit Guaranty Corporation set up in 1974 to oversee private pension plans and to administer those of bankrupt companies that were insured through this program.

Ponzi scheme: A crafty plan in which the people who first enter by paying an amount of money in the hope of a large payoff receive ample financial rewards. As the plan grows and takes in greater numbers of potential recipients, the money received is spread over more and more people until there are not enough funds left to cover everyone.

Privatization (or privatize): A term used in describing the changing of a government system into a program run and administered by a private sector company or corporation.

Regressive tax: A tax that is excessive to the point that it tends to reduce individual savings and/or spendable income.

Social Security Board: The name of the first regulatory body of the Social Security system set up in 1936.

Social Security Trust Funds: The four trust funds set up by the federal government to track the income and payment of monies used and collected under Social Security.

SSI: Supplemental Security Income. The welfare program started in 1987 to provide cash payments for the elderly and those not eligible for Social Security. It receives its funding through the government's annual budget, not through Social Security taxes.

SSIBC: Social Security Investment Banking Corporation. The name of the proposed new system to replace current Social Security.

Third Millennium: A group founded for the younger generation, ages twenty-five to thirty-five, to argue and protest the problems of Social Security.

Thrift ethic: A set of values that makes people understand the duty they have to ourselves to save in order to provide for their future.

Treasury bonds: Nonmarketable bonds issued by the Treasury to the Social Security Trust Funds to account for borrowing all the surplus funds in these accounts.

Trustees Report: The official annual report that the trustees of Social Security release each year showing the condition of Social Security.

TSP: Thrift Savings Plan. A retirement plan for federal employees under FERS based on investment and growth. It is administered by a separate government board. See FERS.

Underfunding (or unfunded): The failure of a pension plan, whether government or private, to have on hand the amount of money needed to handle all future retirement obligations.

Vesting: The conveying to an employee of an inalienable right to share in a pension fund.

Bibliography

Boskin, Michael J. *Too Many Promises.* Homeward, Ill.: Dow Jones-Irwin, 1986.

Church, George J., and Lacayo, Richard. "The Case for Killing Social Security." *Time* (March 20, 1995).

Ferrara, Peter J. "Social Security and Medicare," Washington, D.C.: Cato Institute, 1995.

———. *Social Security: Prospects for Real Reform.* Washington, D.C.: Cato Institute, 1985.

Gross, Martin L. *A Call for Revolution.* New York: Ballantine Books, 1993.

Hardy, Dorcas. *Social Insecurity.* New York: Villard Books, 1991.

Hewitt, Paul. "How AARP Would Bankrupt America," National Taxpayers Union Foundation, Washington (April 28, 1993).

———. "Survey of Retirement Confidence," National Taxpayers Union Foundation, Washington (September 1993).

Karpel, Craig S. *The Retirement Myth.* New York: HarperCollins, 1995.

"Proposals for Alternate Investment of the Social Security Trust Fund Reserves," Hearing—Subcommittee on Social Security, House Ways and Means Committee (October 4, 1994).

Quadagno, Jill. *The Transformations of Old Age Security.* Chicago: University of Chicago Press, 1991.

Robertson, A. Haeworth. "Social Security's Uncertain Future," Washington, D.C.: Cato Institute, 1993.

———. *Social Security: What Every Taxpayer Should Know.* Charlotte, N.C.: Retirement Policy Institute, 1992.

Shipman, William. "Retiring with Dignity: Social Security vs. Private Markets," Washington, D.C.: Cato Institute (August 14, 1995).

Weaver, Carolyn L. (Director, Social Security and Pension Studies). "Social Security Investment Policy," Washington, D.C.: American Enterprise Institute (August 1994).

Weinbach, Lawrence A. (Chair, Subcommittee on Pensions). "Who Will Pay for Your Retirement? The Looming Crisis," New York: Committee for Economic Development, 1995.

Index

AARP (American Association of Retired Persons)
beginnings, 65
Joe Perkins, vice president, 112
maximum benefits from Social Security, 199
revenues, 65
Senate investigation, 65
A Call for Action, 258
Adams, John, 43
AFDC, Aid to families with dependent children, 97, 180
Age, forty or under, 152
Aid to Families with Dependent Children (see AFDC)
Alfange, Dean, 139
Allies, during World War II, 21

Alternate Plan, The, 195, 196, 197, 198, 199
American Association of Retired Persons (see AARP)
American Express Company pension plan, 122, 123, 124
Archer, Bill, congressman, R-Texas, 28, 30, 39, 108, 109
Axis, during World War II, 21

Baby boomers, chapter 5,
aging, 73
association, 83
beginnings, 73, 74
congressional hearings, 77
life expectancy, 83
when retiring, 126

Year 2002, 74
Benefits, 26
Bipartisan Commission on Entitlement and Tax Reform, 38, 62, 90
Board of Governors, SSIBC, chapter 17,
    structure, 237, 238
    duties, 238, 239
Boskin, Michael J., 217
Busboy, future retirement, 209, 210
Business community, 255

C Fund
    compounding, 147
    investments, 146
    payout, 147, 148
Canadian problems, 66
Carnegie, Andrew, 70
CBO (Congressional Budget Office), 77, 82, 187
CED (Committee for Economic Development), 182, 183, 184
Charity Organization Society, 58, 59
Charts
    Social Security, income and outgo, 234
    Thrift Savings Plan, 148
Chevron Oil Company
    Gulf Oil buyout, 115, 116
Chile, social security system, 65
Civil Service Retirement System (see CSRS)
COLAs (cost of living adjustments), 103, 142, 145, 146,
    150, 168
Comments from students, 67, 68
Committee for Economic Development (see CED)
Congress
    changing options, 198
    getting elder vote, 103
    hiding true national debt, 75
    increasing rates, 178
    limited progress, 186
    make changes to Social Security, 177, 178, 183
    mechanisms for new system, 54
    national debt, 43
    new ideas, 193
    operations, 98
    pay-as-you-go system, 54
    PBGC, 138
    raising money for Social Security, 54
    raising retirement age, 76
    retiring, 149, 150
    Social Security, 175
    1992 elections, 73
    1994 elections, 74
Congressional Budget Office (see CBO)
Cost of Living Adjustment (see COLAs)
CPI (Consumer Price Index), 131
CSRS (Civil Service Retirement System), chapter 10,
    benefits, 143
    history, 142
    options, 143

Death benefits, 214
  example, 214, 215
Decker, Bill, 195
Declaration of Independence, 58
Defined benefits plans, 168
Deficit, 35
Democrats,
  actions, 60, 76
  control of Congress, 54, 55
  deficits, 90
  Old Guard, 27
DeVries, Peter, 253
Disabled workers, 214
Dust Bowl, 41

Eastern Airlines, 34
economists, 76
Edward, King of England, 57
Eisenhower, Dwight D., 167
Elders, 74, 107
Entitlements, 25
Entitlements Commission, 62
ERISA, 129
Exemption for government entities,
  52

F Fund, 147
Fannie Maes, 147
Federal Employees Retirement Sys-
  tem (*see* FERS)
Federal retirement, chapter 10, 173
Ferrara, Peter J., 217
FERS (Federal Employees Retire-
  ment Systems), 42
  enacted, 143

examples, 144
parts of plan, 144
FICA, 25, 26, 36, 42, 95, 96
  new direction, 202, 257
  implied compact, 230
Figgie, Harry J. Jr., 106
First Financial Capital Corporation,
  195
Founding Fathers, 41
Funding, Individual Security Retirement Account, 201
  example, 205

G Fund, 146
Galveston, Texas, 24, 202
General Motors,
  underfunding, 117, 118, 119
G.I. Bill, 22
Ginnie Maes, 147
Gold Rush, 34
Gompers, Samuel,
  beliefs, 71, 72
  Socialism, 71
Gornto, Rick, 196, 199
Great Depression, 33
Great Society, 60
Gulf Oil pensions, 115, 116

Hamilton, Alexander, 141
Harrison, Jennifer story, 67, 68
Hewitt, Paul
  congressional hearings, 78, 81
  entitlements, 108, 109
Holbrook, Ray, County Judge, 196,
  197

House Ways and Means Committee, 39
Houston Chronicle,
  Social Security to borrow, 38
  Story on NCSSR, 39
  other stories, 191

Individual Retirement Account (*see* IRA)
Individual Security Retirement Account (*see* ISRA)
Industrial Revolution, 58, 121
Internal Revenue Service (*see* IRS)
IOUs, 36, 37, 42
  U.S. Treasury bonds, 91
IRA (Individual Retirement Account),
  beginnings, 66, 111
  from part of FICA, 63
  idea, 191, 192
IRS (Internal Revenue Service), 251
ISRA (Individual Security Retirement Account), chapter 15,
  current contributions, 203
  dividends, 251
  employers share used for, 220
  estimated retirement amounts, 214
  example withdrawals, 213, 214
  first opened, 263
  funding procedures, 249
  new program, 177
  no new taxes, 178
  price of stock, 263

rates, 178, 179
retirement tables,
  6.5 percent, 205, 206
  8 percent, 207, 208
safeguards, 193
selling shares, 250, 251
stock price increase, 250
tax free, 251
time for purchase, 250
worker's estate, 249

Jacobs, Andy, congressman, D-Ind.
  congressional hearing, 82
Jefferson, Thomas, 33, 51, 73, 87, 95, 247, 270
John, King of England, 57

Kebodeaux, Don, 195, 196, 199
Keith, Hastings, former congressman, 146
Kennedy, John F., 153
Kerrey, Robert, Senator, 38, 62, 63
Klein, James
  congressional hearing, 80

Lexington, Mass., 40
Literary writers remarks, 64
LTV, 125

Magna Carta, 57
Means testing, 164, 222
Medicare rate, 180, 181
Members of Congress
  Archer, Bill, R-Tx, 28, 30, 39, 99, 108, 109

Bunning, Jim, R-Ky, 78, 193
Gingrich, Newt, R-Ga, 190, 191
Jacobs, Andy, D-Ind, 77, 82, 187
Pickle, J. J., D-Tx, 101, 149
Porter, John, R-Il, 63, 82, 186
Meredith, Karen, Founder of AAB, 83
Morgan, J.P., Company, 191

National Commission on Social Security Reform (*see* NCSSR)
National debt, 29, 103
National Taxpayers Union Foundation,
   study of retiring congressmen,
      149, 150
   recommended benefits for
   members of congress, 150
NCSSR (National Commission on
   Social Security Reform), 27,
   28, 30
New Deal, 45, 46
Newspaper accounts of Social Security problems, 181, 182
Notch problem, 232, 233

OASDI (Old-Age Survivors and
   Disability Insurance), chapter 4,
   97
Old Guard, 34
Opting out of Social Security, 195

Pan Am World Airways, 131, 132
PBGC (*see* Pension Benefit Guaranty Corporation)

Penney, J.C.
   workers pension settlement, 116
Pension Benefit Guaranty Corporation (PBGC),
   annual report, 1991, 135
   beginnings, 128, 129
   board of directors, 137
   Braniff Airways, 132
   companies using stock for pen-
      sion plans, 119
   employees of bankrupt plans cov-
      ered, 131
   ERISA (Employee Retirement In-
      come Security Act), 129
   Eastern Airlines, 132
   insurance premiums, 133
   list of underfunded companies,
      130
   1994 new additions to under-
      funded list, 136
   Reagan, Ronald, 185
Pensions, 110
   American Express, 122, 123
   Baltimore & Ohio R.R., 123
   Pennsylvania R.R., 124, 125
   earliest plans, 122, 125
Perot, Ross, 70
Pickle, J.J., congressman, 149
Priddy, Martha, 81
Private sector refunds, 179
   benefits, 257
Privatization, 55
Ponzi scheme, 176
Porter, John, congressman, D-Il, 63,
   82, 190

Public ownership, SSIBC, chapter 18

Relief, 54
Republic Steel, 125
Republicans
  control, 65
Retirees
  earned their retirement, 40, 41
Retirement plans
  Congressman Proter's, 63
  use of taxes, 158
Rockefeller, John D., 70
Roosevelt, Franklin D., 33, 159
  chapter 3, 45
  first hundred days, 46
  intentions, 46
  New Deal, 45
  on the dole thinking, 99
  reason for Social Security, 47
  Social Security Act, 48, 49, 50, 51, 52
Roosevelt, Theodore, 101, 200
Ross, Stanford, 107
Runnymede, England, 57

Savings, 110
SEC (Securities and Exchange Commission), 46
Self-employed, 255
Senate Finance Committee, 102
Senior Citizens Equity Act, 108
Server benefits, 209, 210
Shipman, William D., 189
Simpson, Alan, Senator, R-Wy, 65, 170

Social Security, chapter 4,
  bonds, 91, 92, 93, 94
  COLAs, 63
  congressional choices, 63
  congressional hearings, baby boomers, 80
  copy of original Social Security brochure, 48, 49, 50, 51, 52
  early beginnings, 58
  FICA deductions, 63
  first benefits, 60
  first recipient, 60
  how money is used, 112
  in bad shape, 110
  IOUs, government bonds, 88
  independent agency, 1994, 58, 98, 101
  maximum, 1995–96, 145
  monthly payments, 88
  OASDI, 92
  other countries, 65
  ratios, 61
  Shirley S. Chater, 104
  Social Security Act, 30, 35, 37, 39, 47
  statistics, 62
  surplus, 62, 74
  Title II, 60
  trust funds, 91, 274
  Trustees report, 61, 89
  year 2002, 63
Social Security brochure
  your part of tax, 51
  employers part of tax, 51

Old age reserve account, 52
Social Security Board, 1936, 103
SSI (Supplemental Security Income), 180
SSIBC (Social Security Investment Banking Corporation), chapter 17
State pension plans, chapter 11, 155
Supplemental Security Income (*see* SSI)
Svahn, John, commissioner, 38

Teachers retirement system, Texas, 156, 157
Third Millennium, 183
Thrift Savings Plan, 146, 149
  C Fund, 146, 147
  F Fund, 147
  G Fund, 146
  graph, 148
  investments, 147
  payoffs, 148
Tobias, Andrew, 26, 27
Truman, Harry, S., president, 45
Trust funds, 88, 89
Trustee reports

annual, 62
surplus, 89
interest, 98
TVA, 46, 121

Underfunded
  government pensions, 149
  obligations, 117, 118
  state pensions, 159, 160
United Mine Workers, 128
U.S. Office of Personnel Management, 142

Vesting
  Social Security, 53
  Thrift Savings Plan, 147

Wall Street beginnings, 253, 254
Washington, George, 127
Weaver, Carolyn L., Dr., 188, 189, 190
Welfare, 107
Wilson, Woodrow, 112, 194, 235
World War II, 21, 22, 60

Young, Arthur, 252